# THREE PLAYS

# THREE PLAYS
## by George F. Walker

---

**Bagdad Saloon**
**Beyond Mozambique**
**Ramona and the White Slaves**

**The Coach House Press**
**Toronto**

Copyright © Canada, 1978, George F. Walker

These plays are fully protected by copyright. All inquiries
concerning performing rights, professional or amateur,
readings, or any other use of this material should
be directed to:
Great North Agency Limited
345 Adelaide Street West, Suite 500
Toronto, Ontario M5A 1V9

Photo credits
Bagdad Saloon: Mike Dobel
Beyond Mozambique: (colour slides) Brian Arnott
Ramona and the White Slaves: Andrew Tate

Edited for the press by Martin Kinch.

Set in Times and printed in Canada

The Coach House Press,
401 (rear) Huron Street
Toronto, Canada M5S 2G5

Published with the assistance of the Canada Council
and the Ontario Arts Council.

ISBN 88910-078-0

Third Printing

This book is dedicated to Stephanie Ann Staton

# Contents

# Introduction

*Am I not amazing?* (Rocco, *Beyond Mozambique*)
*Am I not a king?* (Ahrun, *Bagdad Saloon*)


Not many prairie landscapes in George Walker's plays. Or, indeed any of those images that one used to associate with Canadian drama. Walker's settings are exotic: Arabian deserts, African jungles and the seamy ports of Hong Kong. The few Canadian references that do exist, like Lance's preoccupation with wheat in *Beyond Mozambique,* are fiendishly ironic.

Of course, most Canadian playwrights of the 1970s quickly outgrew their self-consciousness with national symbols, but a number of observers found common denominators in the Canadian preference for naturalism. (See *Urjo Kareda's Introduction to Leaving Home* by David French, New Press 1972). Six years later, the *New York Times,* thinking itself very up to date, published an article on Canadian Drama by Henry Popkin (January 15, 1978) which also emphasized 'the realistic bias of Canadian drama ... (and) ... its commitment to Canadian subject matter.'

Not much naturalism in George Walker's plays. They are, in fact, violently anti-naturalistic. One might well ask if Walker is outside the mainstream of recent Canadian playwriting.

*Style. I think it has something to do with style.* (Ahrun, *Bagdad Saloon*)
*European wit? Where did you pick it up?* (Rocco, *Beyond Mozambique*)

Walker's early plays, particularly *Prince of Naples* and *Ambush at Tether's End,* show a distinctly European style, a linguistic wit that pays respect to the French absurdists and the English tradition for articulate language. These plays reflect little, if anything, of the Canadian experience. Two years later, when Walker began *Bagdad Saloon,* the frustrations of trying to create an indigenous theatre in Canada had become very real and immediate. Naturalism and conservatism had quickly taken the field — at least in terms of hit shows and public acceptance — and ambitious, personal statements, such as John Palmer's *Memories for my Brother, part II,* and *Touch of God in the Golden Age* (both of which had a seminal influence on Walker) were totally dismissed and ignored.

After two and one half years of frenetic activity, when the first wave of new Canadian Drama burst forth in the 1970s, two images remained in the forefront of our consciousness at the Factory Theatre Lab where Walker's plays were performed. First the realization that the Canadian cultural field was a desert, a place of shifting fashions, lacking in roots or traditions. Second, a sense of inertia, a recognition of the impossibility of change, and the literal banging of one's head aganst the wall. It is in this context that we must look at *Bagdad Saloon,* which, for all its exotic flavor, is as Canadian as moose meat.

*Dramatics. Dialectics. Sub plots. Nothing happening. But with the greatest amount of fuss. Things begin slowly. Divide themselves into scenes. Going madly in all directions. To avoid the problem itself. Inertia. Non action. No action. No play.* (Ahrun)

*Bagdad Saloon* was written during Walker's first trip abroad in 1972, in a large room on Aynhoe Road in Hammersmith, London. While the work is not consciously political or even sociological, it is nonetheless, an apt metaphor for the building of a new Canadian culture. Ahrun, the mad dreamer, obsessed with cult figures and everyone else's fame, creates a structure to house mythic figures from other countries, notably America. He hopes to achieve renown by placing himself in the company of famous people and learning their secrets.

*Fame is the artist's only excuse for existence.* (Ahrun)
*A great man never dies. He doesn't even fade.* (Doc)

The American heroes are all dismantled. Henry (Miller) is a vainglorious fool chasing his own windmills in the form of the Pulitzer Committee. Expatriate Gertrude Stein is a genius, witty and perceptive, but mad, hopelessly mad. Dolly Stiletto is hardly a heroine by anybody's standards, but she goes on dreaming, placing all her faith in her son as the archetypal hero who can reverse all odds. Doc Halliday, for all his bravado, proves to be a frightened schoolboy, still struggling to learn to read.

But the Americans don't worry about their failings. They carry on. 'Presume that you are famous and let the world prove you wrong,' cries Stein. Ahrun desperately wants more. He believes that fame, however fickle, 'can create things. Purpose. Glamour. Mystique. Artists. Or folk heroes. (...) then folk-lore (...) and more folk-lore ... and then – ....'

It is in this terrifying pause that Ahrun realizes the emptiness of his pursuits.
What is tragic about Ahrun and pathetic about his associate, Aladdin, is that
they can never achieve fame because they worry too much, because they stare
at themselves through other people's eyes.

The play and the universe grow progressively out of control. Chaos reigns.
Dolly's son, the ultimate hero, the big-time winner, proves to be a grotesque
monster-child called Ivanhoe, himself desperately trying to switch careers. In
the final scene, Ahrun, Aladdin and his servant are buried in cobwebs, while the
real mythic figures, fading and rotted, carry on with their banquet, a triumphant
toast to style. Ahrun, the man who wanted substance, is no more.

Walker's own style for *Bagdad Saloon* is bold and panoramic, and his de-
scription of the play as a 'cartoon' tends to belie its thematic density. Walker
explored the cartoon form in his previous play, *Sacktown Rag*, an occasionally
autobiographical retrospection of life in the slummy side of Cabbagetown in the
fifties. The episodic cartoon allows all of Walker's theatrical instincts to break
loose — the form is really a celebration of theatre — and certainly keeps naturalistic tendencies and ordinary stage logic at more than arm's length. It offers
Walker a sprawling canvas on which to paint his themes and even gives the
characters a kind of erratic autonomy to move in and out as they please. The
structure of the play is very simple. In the first part, the saloon is artificially
constructed, crassly decorated with singing masonettes, then peopled with
cultural artifacts. The second part dismantles the structure and destroys the
'culture' in favor of general chaos.

The Factory was filled with chaos itself prior to the Bagdad premiere, and
nearly collapsed after its mammoth Works Festival in December, 1972, which
resulted in a major dispute with Actors Equity. *Bagdad Saloon* came within ten
minutes of not making it into rehearsal, but finally the bank yielded, and the
show proved an important breakthrough for Walker, paving the way for his next
work, *Beyond Mozambique*.

*There is a tower growing in the jungle. It is the power of light and the shrewd mind of
darkness. It is the culmination of all history and civilization, and it is turning my mind to
soup.* (Rocco, *Beyond Mozambique*)

In it's initial draft, *Beyond Mozambique* also borrowed from the long, sprawling form of *Bagdad Saloon*. But Walker grew dissatisfied with much of it during a workshop exploration of the play and condensed it into a tighter framework. Although very funny, *Beyond Mozambique* is murkier and more obsessive than *Bagdad Saloon,* and marks the beginning of a painful, interior descent for Walker.

Ahrun, at least had the realization that action was only possible within a moral context:

*Morality. (...) The scale of man's shortcomings ranging from greed to petty malice is all defined by the one ultimate evil in him. The ability to destroy his fellows. This obliterates everything. And, therefore, a moral man must act.* (Pause) *Action. One more chance.* (Pause) *Act. ...* (Pause)

It is too late for Ahrun and he is forced to face his own hollowness. But Rocco, the Italian doctor from *Beyond Mozambique,* is beyond morality. Buried in the deep jungle, the bowels of the earth, he is able to exorcise his conscience by keeping busy with Frankenstein-ish experiments. He is haunted by his past life as a butcher in a Nazi hospital, but his obsession with his own work wins out. Besides, Rocco recognizes in himself a mirror of the world. 'There is something about committing crimes against humanity that puts you in touch with the purpose of the universe,' he declares. He is intent on becoming a force of darkness — more depraved and therefore less dangerous than the Zastrozzi of Walker's later work — but nonetheless a universal force on par with God and Ignorance.

Yet while Rocco can wryly call himself 'the absence of God,' he also eventually admits his work is his penance. 'It's not fame, I'm after, but redemption.'

The other characters are equally haunted and desperate, if less lofty in their obsession. Lance wants to redeem himself in his dead father's eyes; Rita wants to make a non-porno movie; Liduc will settle for a single convert for Jesus; and Olga wants simply to savour her dreams. But it is Rocco who can most calmly face and manipulate the ultimate cataclysm that awaits them.

*I have finally destroyed that fucking tower.* (Rocco)
*I can't see no fucking mountain.* (Gloria, *Ramona and the White Slaves*)

Like Tom Stoppard (whose writing Walker's most clearly relates to). Walker would probably claim to have no social or political statements to make, and the scintillating writing style would support that claim. Yet all three plays point to a world that is clearly at the point of collapse. What is most frightening about the world of Mozambique is its hilarious flirtation with destruction. 'I don't understand how you make all this violence seem so gratuitous,' jokes Father LiDuc, after scenes that include dismemberment and rape. This may reflect some of the darker recesses of Walker's mind – his next play, *Ramona,* grows even darker – but it is also, I think, a concern for a society that has grown out of touch with reality. A social revolution *is* taking place in the jungle and the neurotic white trash are being driven back into their cages in the final assault of the play.

*Prophecy is an escape from memory. Now what the hell does that mean?* (Lance)
*Jesus doesn't mind losers, but he has no patience with idiots.* (LiDuc)

While *Beyond Mozambique* is the most direct and clearest of Walker's plays in this trilogy, it was probably the least understood in its first production in 1974. It was negatively reviewed by most critics, and Urjo Kareda, writing in the Star, was simply baffled: 'the play may be a subversive report to the Canada Council,' he ventured. The producion drew respectable crowds, probably due to the presence of Frances Hyland and Donald Davis in the cast, but the response could hardly be called overwhelming. Even the Arts Councils were unhappy with the production and Factory grants were frozen that year.

Walker became more removed and introspective for a period, and it became difficult for him to write his next play, *Ramona and the White Slaves.* It wasn't just the fact that critics didn't like his work (except for *Prince of Naples,* Walker had grown used to generally weak critical response), but rather it was the realization that he still didn't have a context in which to explore his most important unconventional themes and style. He toyed with the idea of writing novels, where it seemed easier to work in a vacuum. He wrote a first draft of a naturalistic ('I can do it too') play called 'Decades.' He and Stephanie Staton (his lady during all this period) bought a truck and travelled to Las Vegas, California and Vancouver. When I met him in Abbotsford, B.C., a year after *Beyond Mozambique* had opened, he had only written a few scenes of a long, epic version of *Ramona.* The play was, as always, fascinating in its design, but confused and tentative in its approach. We had a very odd conversation about

Canadian theatre at the St. Benedictine monastery overlooking the Fraser Valley.

In any case, Walker found a way of dealing with the vacuum, and, in the summer of 1975, wrote *Ramona* in the backyard of an East End Toronto house. On a scene to scene basis, I think the play contains his finest writing. Again, he compressed the play into a tighter form than originally conceived, but, with its opium nightmare structure, its short, episodic scenes that jump through time zones, it provided Walker ample room to probe the bewildering mind of its title character. It's not a pleasant play. Though not without Walker's usual ironic humour, it is much less funny then his other works. Ramona is a *man* beyond morals, a vicious bitch goddess, supreme manipulator, whose torments to others are not designed for pleasure or even personal gain. Unlike Olga, she achieves no secret sexual twinges from others' pain, and, despite an over-whelming Catholic background, shows no traces of guilt. In fact, she has moved beyond guilt, thought punishment, and into oblivion. She is a Medean figure, a cannibal, who devours her children to keep them at home, and who slices apart the men who have failed her. The play is a dark journey into the soul of a woman who doesn't much like herself, yet who uses drugs to help herself remember her own scars. But she is charming too, articulate and seductive, mirroring too well the society around her. *However,* it is not the world that is exploding here. The wars taking place beyond Hong Kong seem trivial compared to the clinical destruction of the family unit that Romana brings about.

*Ramona and the White Slaves* creates problems for its audiences, although the essential narrative is revealed unequivocally on the last page: 'The story of a family and Miguel's deterioration and how small he became and how he changed disguises ...' This is the mystery that Detective Cook has been trying to unravel throughout; in the role he is a barometer the audience can relate to. He helps us distinguish reality from hallucination, and past from present. But then the actor playing Cook also plays Sebastian, who turns out to be Miguel. Cook and Sebastian are clearly two distinct characters, but one is less certain about Freddie and Mitch, who are also played by a single actor. Then there is the complication of Ramona and Sebastian suddenly switching roles in one of the final scenes, which, while it provides some clarifying expositon, leaves the audience agape trying to figure out what's going on. Personally, I find this scene glib and overextended, detracting from the rhythm of a cascading series of horrific revelations. But because Walker capsulizes the story so clearly at the end, he may want to confuse the audience at this point and force us to deal with blurred borderlines.

Some of the fault may lie in the original production, which was, in fact, a difficult first directing assignment for the author. Another production is needed to resolve the question of the final scenes. Nonetheless, the play remains masterful in its use of language, its economy, and its mysterious revelation of unnatural human behaviour.

*Ramona and the White Slaves* was also poorly received, and this may have prodded Walker to write two works in a more popular vein, *Gossip* and *Zastrozzi,* both for Toronto Free Theatre. *Gossip* failed in its original production, but six months later proved a surprise critical and popular hit in Seattle. In fact, Walker has had three hit productions in as many months. *Zastrozzi,* which opened in November, 1977 at Toronto Free Theatre was the first Walker play to receive unanimous rave responses, and the revival of *Beyond Mozambique* at the Factory, directed by the author, was also a hit. Either the desert is becoming more hospitable, or audiences may have simply learned to tune in to Walker's unique style.

The publication of these works lends a permanence to the transient nature of their production history. The three plays reflect the most important period in Walker's writing career so far, but, while a distinct unity, the trilogy does not feel complete. Walker is too humanistic to end with Ramona's seductive but amoral final posture. Another grappling with the desert itself seems imminent and will probably find its resolution in a new play, *The Desert's Revenge,* a return to the panoramic form of *Bagdad Saloon.*

It is clear that for all of his dark preoccupations, Walker wants an audience and wants to entertain. To watch George Walker at the opening of one of his own plays is a rare treat. Aside from the endless pacing and peering behind audience risers, as the audience inevitably breaks into laughter, one can see Walker's eyes widen and the face break into a broad, helpless grin.

KEN GASS, FACTORY THEATRE LAB
*January, 1978*

# BAGDAD SALOON

## A Cartoon

*Bagdad Saloon* was first produced at Factory Theatre Lab, Toronto, March 28, 1973, with the following cast:

AHRUN  Michael Ayoub
SARA  Robin Beckwith
HENRY  David Bolt
MITCH  David Clement
JOHN (DOC) HALLIDAY  Dean Hawes
DOLLY STILLETTO  Gale Garnett
ALADDIN  Jim Henshaw
IVANHOE JONES  Guy LaPrade
SERVANT  Howard Mawson
STEIN  Doris Lloyd Petrie
THE MASONETTES  Nancy Ahern, Ann Gourley, Sandy Phillips
THE PIANO PLAYER  George Bassingthwaighte

Directed by:  Eric Steiner
Set Design by:  Doug Robinson
Costumes by:  Shawn Kerwin

*Original Songs*
Music by:  Steven Jack
Lyrics by:  George F. Walker

*Bagdad Saloon* had a subsequent production at the Bush
Theatre, England, October, 1973 – Factory Theatre Lab's
London Tour – with the following cast:

AHRUN   Neil Vipond
SARA   Robin Beckwith
HENRY   David Bolt
MITCH   Don McQuarrie
JOHN (DOC) HALLIDAY   Dean Hawes
DOLLY STILLETO   Brenda Donohue
ALADDIN   David Fox
IVANHOE JONES   Jim Henshaw
SERVANT   Howard Mawson
STEIN   Doris Lloyd Petrie
THE MASONETTES   Patricia Carrol Brown, Carole Zorro,
   Joy Coghill
THE PIANO PLAYER   George Basingthwaighte

Directed by:  Eric Steiner
Set Design by:  Doug Robinson
Costumes by:  Shawn Kerwin

*Persons*
AHRUN  (55 - 65)
ALADDIN  (55 - 65)
SARA  (13 says she's 10)
MITCH
DOLLY STILLETTO
JOHN (DOC) HALLIDAY
STEIN
HENRY
SERVANT
IVANHOE JONES
THE MASONETTES  (Three young ladies)
THE PIANO PLAYER*  (And his piano)

*Can play bridge music until Scene 12.
Then can be incorporated into 'saloon'.

### Prologue

*Cacophony. Shadows. Trumpet calls. Arabian pop music. Singing. Banging. A great din.*

*The entire cast taking part.*

*Building.*

**AHRUN** *enters. Wearing a very plain business suit. A large red tie. All enthused by the activity. Carrying a chair. Smiling.*

*When he sits in the chair he shouts the word 'action.' There is immediate silence.*

*He looks around. Frowns. Stands. Looks around some more. Sits. Smiles.*

AHRUN    Action. Call it a through line. One man. Me. Wanting to be the hero of the piece. Wanting to act and act well. Or failing to act, act that well as well. Hero. Anti-hero. Failed-hero. Action. Acting. Actor.

    [**SARA** *brings out* **AHRUN**'s *costume — his robes. He refuses*]

*[Blackout]*

# Part 1, Scene 1

AHRUN *is standing behind his easel. Examining his canvas. It is empty.* ALADDIN *sits cross-legged. Quietly talking to his pigeons.*

AHRUN   [*vaguely*] Soliloquy. [*Reflects. Pivots*] Then I came to a great and sullen river. It was dreadful as hell. And near it were many haggard figures of the road. Some mildly decaying and others who were noxious and hideously covered in blotches. I asked: What river is this? And was told that it was the river of tears that men shed in lamentation for their dead. I found also that everything was proportionate and that those who stood longer and were more decayed were the sons of the more wasted and vile who had died. And those who shed but a few tears and then passed on were the sons of the dead who were closer to goodness or creation. I sat awhile. Then I noticed a cluster of men in the background who seemed rooted to the earth by dust and who were by far the most hideous of all; and whose skins were full of gaping filthy blotches and whose limbs were bone-thin and crooked. Who are the men in that unfortunate cluster, I asked. And was told — they are the sons of the west.

ALADDIN   That was wonderful.

AHRUN   Thank you. I made it up, you know.

ALADDIN   Wonderful.

      [*Pause.* SARA *enters. A sack over her shoulder*]

SARA   Were you going to go without food?

ALADDIN   I didn't think.

SARA   Stupidity. I've never seen such stupidity. [*She starts off*]

AHRUN   Where are you going?

SARA   Back to bed.

AHRUN   Stay where you are.

SARA   Father. It's late. I'm tired.

AHRUN   You must remain where you are until I give you permission to remain somewhere else.

SARA   Stupidity.

ALADDIN   May I go now?

AHRUN   I'm waiting for the inspiration.

SARA     He's waiting for inspiration.

ALADDIN     Good.

AHRUN     Quick. Everyone look up. [*They look up*] Look at it. Notice the strange shape. Prepare yourself, Aladdin. The shape is just right. The profile of my grandfather.

SARA     Stupidity.

ALADDIN     Wait. I can't find my glasses.

AHRUN     My grandfather's chin. And there's his neck. There was only one neck like that. Go, Aladdin. You will get there all right.

ALADDIN     I see. Yes. I see.

AHRUN     Good. Begin your odyssey.

ALADDIN     I'm on my way.

SARA     You can't send him on an odyssey. He's not the type.

AHRUN     Profiles of ancestors in the moon. Directly preceding great achievements. A family omen.

SARA     What profile? That's a full moon.

AHRUN     You aren't looking closely enough. Get going, Aladdin.

ALADDIN     I am on my way. I will send you a pigeon.

AHRUN     Yes. Yes. Send me as many as you want. But get going.

ALADDIN     Good-bye. [*To* SARA] Nothing bad will happen to me. I'm too innocent. [*He leaves*]

SARA     He doesn't have a chance.

AHRUN     It's a long time since any of us did anything so worthwhile. And worthwhile things must be done in the most difficult way. He is very fortunate. And also courageous.

SARA     He's senile. He doesn't know whether he's coming or going. He thinks he's got the power of the magic lamp.

AHRUN     Why not. His ancestors had it.

SARA     Hog wash. I'm going back to bed. [*She leaves*]

AHRUN     You have my permission to go back to bed.
      [*Notices that she has left. Sighs*]
    A pathetic fallacy. A conspiracy to make me seem constantly mediocre. [*Looking up*] Just the hint of a profile would have been enough. Why is it that I cannot be anything more than mundane. [*Pause*] Am I not a king?

[*Blackout*]

## Part 1, Scene 2

MITCH *enters. Wearing a tuxedo. Vaguely Chinese. Carrying a bouquet of flowers. A flask of bourbon strung around his neck.*

MITCH    The fuss is over. Dust has settled on the American dream. The American woman has survived. This year's theme is Oriental Grace. Contestant number thirty-two is from the State of Arizona. Miss Dolly Stilletto.
[DOLLY *enters shyly. Wearing a bulky, cheap fur coat*] Dolly was chosen last year from over fifty other western beauties to represent her state at this pageant. Weren't you Dolly?

DOLLY    Yes.

MITCH    'The flowers shine like her face, the spring winds sweep the balustrade, the dew lies heavy.' [*Smiles*] From a poem by Li Po.

DOLLY    It's lovely.

MITCH    Say hello to the judges, Dolly.

DOLLY    Hello. [*Pause*]

MITCH    Hey, why are you wearing that big ole coat, kiddo?

DOLLY    Well ...

MITCH    The king's gardeners are picking flowers. The brightest petals will be chosen. Nobody takes a bush to the palace. Take it off.

DOLLY    [*slowly undoing the buttons*] I want to tell you how wonderful it feels to be here. All year long I've been looking forward to this pageant.

MITCH    Humility catches us off guard.
[*Gestures for her to remove coat. She takes it off.* DOLLY *is very pregnant.* MITCH *looks up. Pauses. Reaches into his pocket. Takes out a small book. Will refer to it occasionally*]

DOLLY    I don't want to be disqualified.

MITCH    Contestant thirty-three is from the State of Virginia.
[*The first* MASONETTE *comes on*]

DOLLY    You're not finished with me yet.

MITCH    Move on and make room for thirty-three, thirty-two.

DOLLY    No. I'm gonna do my tricks first.

MITCH    Force will be met with force.

DOLLY    This year's theme is Oriental Grace.

MITCH    Yes. Of course. And it is an ill wind which carries absolutely no good at all.

DOLLY  I'm going to walk up the ramp. Turn around a couple of times
       and let everyone have a good look. [*She proceeds to do so*] Stop.
       Pose. Turn around. Pose again.
MITCH  Delicate conversation. Good manners. The fear of God. Contes-
       tant number thirty-four is from the State of Ohio. She has taken
       on a new name. A Pakistani name which I cannot pronounce, but
       which means ... Still Waters.
            [*Second* MASONETTE *comes on*]
DOLLY  I'm not ashamed of being pregnant. And that's half the battle,
       isn't it? Strike. Strike the pose.
MITCH  Low-key. Soft sell. Subtle variations. And the gradual shift in
       trends.
DOLLY  This is my first child. I was born in 1840, and I'm well over one
       hundred years old. It's been a difficult pregnancy. But my pos-
       ture's still pretty good. Pose.
MITCH  Contestant number thirty-five is from Arkansas. She wants us to
       tell you that she is a recent convert to Buddhism.
            [*Third* MASONETTE *comes on*]
DOLLY  I'm going to give birth to a very special person. I had my tea cup
       read in New Orleans.
MITCH  Buddhism is a religion which elevates the status of mankind.
       Man must answer to himself and not to a supernatural agency.
       We are all very proud of number thirty-five.
            [DOLLY *stiffens with pain. Sighs*]
DOLLY  He knows it's going to be tough without a father.
MITCH  [*on the edge of catatonia*] Numbers thirty-six through forty are all
       members of an obscure Indian caste studying the strange
       metamorphosis of the Asian Moth.
DOLLY  [*to* MITCH] I need a man. My baby needs a man.
MITCH  They believe that one of these moths is the son of God.
            [HENRY *enters. Approaches* MITCH]
HENRY  Excuse me. Can you help me? I'm supposed to deliver a speech.
MITCH  Not now. No ... not now. [*Stares off*]
DOLLY  [*to* HENRY] Are you the father of my baby?
HENRY  No. Doc Halliday is the father of your baby. You always refused
       to sleep with me. Probably because you thought I didn't have
       much talent.
DOLLY  Henry, don't ever talk to me like that again. I'm old enough to be

your grandmother.

MITCH  The Oriental influence is running rampant. Things have changed for the better.

HENRY  [*to* DOLLY] I'm being considered for the Pulitzer Prize, you know. That's why this speech is so important.

MITCH  Not now.

HENRY  I know who *she* is. Who are *you?*

MITCH  Nobody.

HENRY  I'm a bit confused. I think I'll go away and think things over.

[*As* HENRY *is leaving,* STEIN *enters carrying two suitcases. Drops them. Snaps her fingers at* HENRY]

STEIN  Come along boy. I have a boat to catch.

HENRY  I'm not your lackey, Stein. I have a speech to memorize.

MITCH  No, no. Go away, Stein. Go away.

STEIN  [*to* HENRY] Who's he?

HENRY  Nobody.

STEIN  Tell him he fits the part.

HENRY  Now listen ...

STEIN  Pick up my bags, you snivelling non-entity. And follow me to the docks.

HENRY  I am laughing at you Stein. On the outside I may appear flaccid, but inside I am laughing at you. [HENRY *leaves*]

STEIN  That man is a hack. Have you read any of his books. Demented hack. Thinks that a religious theme is having someone urinate in a church. [*Pause*] Not a cathedral mind you. A church.

[MITCH *gestures for* STEIN *to follow* HENRY. STEIN *shrugs.* MITCH *tries to gather his faculties*]

MITCH  We are fast approaching the twenty-first century. And life in our great nation goes progressively on.

STEIN  Well it will have to go on without me. I'm going to Paris and I'm never coming back.

DOLLY  Paris. I was there once.

STEIN  You deserve everything bad that has ever happened to you. Although I don't know you personally I have an intuitive grasp on the causes of all misfortune.

DOLLY  My baby needs a man. Can you help me.

STEIN  No. I don't know any men. All I know are frustrated saints and gods. [*To* MITCH] You boy. Take these bags to the pier.

MITCH   No. We've been interrupted. I've been interrupted. There is still much to say about cultures blending and so on. Our future. Our glory ...

STEIN   Glory.

DOLLY   Glory.

STEIN   Fame is within our grasp. We're all young and talented. But for glory a person has to really sweat.

DOLLY   Horses sweat. Men perspire. Ladies glow.

STEIN   Quaint.

MITCH   May we continue? Will you leave?

STEIN   No.

MITCH   This was my big chance for the limelight. I could become resentful.

STEIN   Pick up my bags. Or I'll tell everyone the disgusting truth about you.

MITCH   Okay. [*They start off*]

STEIN   [*to* DOLLY] I recognize you, you know. You're that cowboy's mistress. Take some advice. If it's exposition you're delivering, don't bother. If it's sympathy you're after, give up. Nobody cares. You're not quite well enough known. You're just as bad off that way as Mr. Nobody my porter here. Bad luck, eh? [*They leave*]

DOLLY   I'm over one hundred years old. I'm pregnant. I came here for fame. Give it to me. Never mind. My child will be a champion. [*Looks around*] Do I win by disqualification?

[*Blackout*]

## Part 1, Scene 3

*AHRUN is standing beside a table. He is drifting. On the table is a typewriter.*

AHRUN   Visions begin slowly. Divide themselves into scenes. Often drifting beyond my grasp. Often. Drifting. Drifting. *[Pause]* And meanwhile I wait to become the hero.
[SERVANT *enters. A budgie on his wrist*]

SERVANT   Excuse me.

AHRUN   You are excused. [SERVANT *leaves.* AHRUN *doesn't notice*]
Type the following. Dearest Aladdin. Old and trusted friend. We have located Stein in Europe. Leave her to me. You are to move west in a suitable disguise.
[SERVANT *comes back on*]

SERVANT   I became momentarily baffled.

AHRUN   That budgie on your wrist.

SERVANT   From Aladdin. A piece of paper was attached to its leg.

AHRUN   What did it say.

SERVANT   Nothing. It was blank.

AHRUN   Say something soothing to me.

SERVANT   Have patience, sir. You'll achieve what you rightly deserve to achieve.

AHRUN   Fair enough.

*[Blackout]*

## Part 1, Scene 4

DOC HALLIDAY. *He stands more or less erect. Fiddling with his gun.* MITCH *enters. Pushing a corpse on a table covered with a sheet.* DOC *is startled. Recovers.*

MITCH     Are you Doc Halliday?
DOC     Why?
MITCH     They say you killed this man.
DOC     Who's 'they'?
MITCH     Everyone. Are you Doc Halliday?
DOC     Who's 'everyone'?
MITCH     Did you kill this man?
DOC     Who are you?
MITCH     [*refers to his book. Puts it away*] Undertaker. [*Lifting sheet*] Do you recognize him?
DOC     Uh-huh.
MITCH     What's his name?
DOC     His name's John Halliday. Some people called him Doc.
MITCH     Oh no you don't. You're Doc Halliday. They told me so.
DOC     They're liars. He's Doc Halliday.
MITCH     Are you sure?
DOC     Have you ever been shot in the stomach?
MITCH     Is this an idle threat? [DOC *draws his gun*]
DOC     What's his name?
MITCH     John Halliday.
DOC     Good. Now what are you gonna put on his tombstone?
MITCH     What do you want me to put on it?
DOC     Here lies Doc Halliday. Dead. Dead but never forgotten. A man who had real balls. Shot in the back by a dirty little cuckold, who didn't have any balls at all.
MITCH     Shot in the back.
DOC     Dead. But never forgotten.
MITCH     Yes. How can I verify this?
DOC     You can ask me. [*Pause*]
MITCH     I understand.
DOC     Good. [MITCH *rushes off with the corpse*] So long, Doc, A great man never dies. He doesn't even fade. [*Chuckles*]

[*Blackout*]

# Part 1, Scene 5

AHRUN *standing. The* SERVANT *at the table next to him. Typing.*
*In either shorthand or Arabic, i.e., one peck per sentence.*

AHRUN *[dictating]* The usual salutation. *[Pause]* What's wrong. What about our plans. Our plots. Where are the results. Have you lost your glasses. Is your arthritis bothering you. Remember you're only as old as you feel. Delete that. Remember that you are a mythic figure in your own right. Delete that. Listen, old friend, I ... I don't quite know what to tell him.

SERVANT Tell him to get on with it.

AHRUN Yes. You must get on with it, Aladdin. Because if you do not get on with it then nothing will happen and we'll disappear for ever. All of us. You too. Me especially. Delete that.

SERVANT Tell him about the rumour.

AHRUN Yes. There is a rumour from somewhere that the one called Doc Halliday is still somehow alive. You are to ignore all the tombstones bearing his name. Find him. And bring him along. Anything else?

SERVANT Can't you think for yourself?

AHRUN I'm preoccupied.

SERVANT Well news from home is always encouraging. Perhaps a humorous anecdote.

AHRUN Oh yes. *[Pause]* We were able to lure Stein by assuring her that the literary trend here these days was cubism, and that she was on the verge of being deified. She arrived one humid morning declaring that this was just the right place for things to pretend to begin when in fact they were just continuing to end, yawned in my face and then sat down on my dead wife's autograph book which she had arrogantly mistaken for a leather foot stool. Weeks and months have passed and she has refused to speak any more to me. I think she calls me racist names behind my back. This whole affair would easily turn into an act of revenge. We must watch. Closing for now. I remain.

SERVANT *[finishes typing]* How will we get it to him.

AHRUN You'll take it to him.

SERVANT Where?

AHRUN New York.

SERVANT    I ask to be excused on account of old age.
AHRUN      Denied. Old age is inexcusable. That's the problem.
SERVANT    What's the problem?
AHRUN      New York. Carnegie Hall. He'll be there. Travel lightly. Good-
           bye.
           [SERVANT *stands. Takes paper from typewriter. Starts off left.*
           *Stops. Starts off right. Stops. Thinks. Goes off left.* SARA *enters.*
           *Carrying* AHRUN'*s robes*]
SARA       Are you ready to put these on yet?
AHRUN      No.
SARA       When?
AHRUN      In time.
SARA       Why not now?
AHRUN      The focus is not right. When the focus is on me, I'll put them on.
SARA       Stubbornness.
AHRUN      Patience.
SARA       Too much trouble. [*She starts off*]
AHRUN      I have read many philosophers. They all say a lot of different
           things. But none of them says that a man should live his life with
           the intent purpose of being forgotten as soon as possible.
           Trouble. The one real trouble for intelligent men is the fear of
           being anonymous. Fame is the only excuse for existence. Take
           me for example. If I had been born in California I would already
           be a legend in my own time. A cult figure.
SARA       What makes you think so.
AHRUN      Those poems I wrote when I was younger. The ones about sand
           storms and death by dehydration.
SARA       You weren't born in California. Too bad. Too bad for all potential
           cult figures who weren't born in California.
AHRUN      I feel a vision coming on. Style. I think it has something to do
           with style.
SARA       Like Al Jolson?
AHRUN      How old are you?
SARA       Ten.
AHRUN      I married your mother when she was nine. Tradition being what
           it was, she never uttered a sound to me until she was twenty-
           seven. Think about that for awhile.
SARA       Think about it yourself.

[*Blackout*]

# Part 1, Scene 6

DOC HALLIDAY *is whittling a piece of wood as he sits semi-leisurely in an old chair.* DOLLY *entering, pushing a pram.*

DOLLY   Now remember, sugar, when he looks at you frown for all you're worth. [*Sees* DOC] There he is, puddin'. The miserable bugger who planted you in my belly.

DOC   Lower your voice, woman.

DOLLY   Stand up! And look your son in the eye.

DOC   Don't have no son.

DOLLY   You deny it. You deny it right in front of him!

DOC   I told you to lower your voice.

DOLLY   Oh you pitiful consumptive. You dare deny him when he can hear you. Pitiful, pitiful skinny-legged man.
    [*She knocks him down*]

DOC   Goddamn it.

DOLLY   Get on your feet.

DOC   Goddamn it. Did anyone see you do that?

DOLLY   Who cares. You're keeping your son waiting.
    [DOC *gets up. Looks around*]

DOC   Crazy woman. Jesus, Dolly, you're lucky you're a woman.

DOLLY   Sure I am. It's the best thing that ever happened to me. Here's the proof. [DOC *adjusts himself. Looks into the pram*]

DOC   Why's he making that face?

DOLLY   He hates you.

DOC   Oh, he can't be more than a few months old.

DOLLY   He learns fast. He hates you 'cause he knows you're a weakling. Stare him down, sugar.

DOC   He's smiling.

DOLLY   He's frowning.

DOC   I tell you he's smiling. That's a smile.

DOLLY   Don't you tell me what's on his face. I know what's on his face — it's a frown. Idiot. I know when he's frowning. I'm his mother.

DOC   Well I say he's smiling. I say he's happy as hell to see me. And I'm his father.

DOLLY   So you admit it. You hear that — he admits it. We don't care. I suppose next you'll be saying you want to visit him occasionally.

DOC       Can't.

DOLLY     And then after that you'll probably want to move in. Set up
          house.

DOC       Nope.

DOLLY     I knew you'd come around. But we're not forgetting the way you
          deserted us. You have to beg.

DOC       Beg?

DOLLY     Beg. Just a little.

DOC       Nothing's changed.

DOLLY     Oh. He won't beg, sugar. Well, it's a lot to ask isn't it? What
          should we do? [To DOC] He says you don't have to beg.

DOC       Nothing's changed.

DOLLY     Didn't you hear me, John. He says you don't have to beg. He
          says you just have to ask.

DOC       Are you gonna keep him?

DOLLY     What!

DOC       I'm sorry.

DOLLY     Of course I'm gonna keep him. What did you expect?

DOC       Didn't expect nothin'.

DOLLY     Did you expect me to sell him? [DOC shrugs] Or maybe you
          expected me to give him to you, to be used as collateral in one of
          your poker games.

DOC       All right. Shut up.

DOLLY     Well, what makes you think you can intimidate me, mister. To
          me you're just a diseased and foolish man that I can knock down
          at will. Remember, I've seen you naked. I've seen you hide in
          closets and run like mad from your own shadow. [To baby] It's
          true, son. There's a real man behind this legend.

DOC       What are you calling him?

DOLLY     His name is Ivanhoe.

DOC       Please change it.

DOLLY     It's Ivanhoe!

DOC       But it's a name for a fop.

DOLLY     It's a hero's name! But that's none of your bloody business, is it?
          We were willing to ignore your thousand shortcomings and all
          you had to do was nod your head. On top of everything else,
          John, you're very stupid. [She starts off with the pram]

DOC       You'll get married to a grocer or minister or something.

DOLLY    Bugger yourself. I'm tired of making excuses for men's problems that I had nothing to do with causing. With Ivanhoe I can start from scratch. Good-bye. [*A few steps. Stops*] Will you miss me?

DOC    No, I don't think so.

[DOLLY *leaves.* DOC *stares after them awhile*]
You'll see. Before he's ten years old, she'll see ... Ivanhoe. [*Sits. Enter* ALADDIN. *Wearing a kilt. A tam. Carrying bagpipes*]

ALADDIN    That was eighty years ago. Doc Halliday the infamous killer is now eighty years older. True, he does not appear to have aged at all. But I think I have found the reason for this. It is because he — like so many Americans of this type — is immortal. He has killed from nineteen to thirty men with his revolver. The count varies with geography. The further east you are the more he has killed. And vice versa to the west. But stranger — it seems that he has been killed four or five times himself. Also I have heard that he has died three times of consumption and on a couple of occasions attempted suicide. And succeeded. [*Sighs*] It is a curious phenomenon — immortality. Curious. I wonder what happens to the progeny of these immortalists. I wonder. Do they age and in fact become older than their parents? Confusing. Or is immortality hereditary. Also confusing. Questions. Why do I ask myself so many questions. I am not even by nature a curious man. And I have no time to answer these questions even if I was. And besides I don't care. I am homesick. And also, I have work to do. [*Shakes his head. Goes over to* DOC. *Produces a small bottle of brown liquid from his coat and shoves it under* DOC's *nose*] MacLaddin's Elixir. The cure-all that everyone's been praying for. [DOC *looks up. Looks down. Stands*] It's a lovely day, isn't it?

DOC    Take that thing off your head.

ALADDIN    Why?

DOC    Just do as I say.

[ALADDIN *shrugs. Removes his tam.* DOC *takes his hat off. Puts it on* ALADDIN's *head*]

ALADDIN    Thank you.

DOC    Have you got any identification?

ALADDIN    I have a passport.

| | |
|---|---|
| DOC | Give it to me. |
| ALADDIN | Why? |
| DOC | I hate being asked questions. Just give it to me. |
| | [ALADDIN *produces his passport, hands it to* DOC. DOC *slaps* ALADDIN *across the face with it*] |
| ALADDIN | Why did you do that? |
| DOC | Don't worry about it. It's a fair trade. Here, take this. |
| | [*Handing* ALADDIN *his wallet*] |
| ALADDIN | Oh I don't want your wallet. |
| DOC | Shut up and put it in your pocket. [ALADDIN *obeys*] |
| ALADDIN | What now? |
| DOC | You can close your eyes if you want. |
| | [ALADDIN *shrugs. Closes his eyes.* DOC *draws his gun —puts it at* ALADDIN's *heart. Cocks the trigger.* ALADDIN *opens his eyes*] |
| ALADDIN | You're going to shoot me. |
| DOC | Uh-huh. |
| ALADDIN | Why? |
| DOC | None of your business. |
| ALADDIN | I see. |
| DOC | If you're worrying about the pain. Don't. I'm going for the heart. You'll feel a thud — then nothing. Ready? |
| ALADDIN | Well, there's just one question. |
| DOC | I don't answer questions. |
| ALADDIN | It's my — Elixir — this ... |
| DOC | What about it? |
| ALADDIN | [*nervously*] People refuse to buy without tasting and having tasted refuse to buy. I myself can't find anything wrong with the taste. But — well you see I would dread dying in such an ignorant condition. |
| DOC | I told ya to make it short. |
| ALADDIN | Could you taste it for me? |
| DOC | No. |
| ALADDIN | Do you believe in God? |
| DOC | Don't know. |
| ALADDIN | Heaven? |
| DOC | Don't know. |
| ALADDIN | I'm an agnostic myself. Still I do believe in a supernatural power |

which is a lot more than you can say for most agnostics.

DOC   Close your eyes.

ALADDIN   Listen, you do this for me and I'll put in a good word for you with whatever unknown power I happen to come across. I promise. Call it an obsession. Call it a passion. Call it a ...

DOC   All right. Hand it over.

ALADDIN   Oh, thank you. A good word. My promise.

DOC   Ah, crap on your promise. I just got thirsty all of a sudden.

ALADDIN   Drink as much as you want.

DOC   I will. [*He pulls the cork out. Drinks. A long drink*]

ALADDIN   Thank you. [*Pause*]

DOC   It stinks. [*Drops the bottle. Raises his gun. Sinks to his knees*] Ah, shit. [*Passes out*]

ALADDIN   [ALADDIN *picks up* DOC's *legs as if to drag him off*] Poor witless creature. Cowardly man. Ass of a pig. Why should you be so well known?

[*Blackout*]

## Part 1, Scene 7

MITCH *wheels the corpse's table on. Sees us. Stops.*

MITCH    [*out front*] I'm all grown up and I still don't know what I want to
be. I can't bury this man. There's too much doubt about his
identity. That's a lie. This is the truth. I have a certain amount of
pull. I could bury him if I wanted to. But I want to stir things up a
bit. Once he's underground he's of no use to anyone. At least
now he's available for mass confusion. Why not. It's all folly. So
I come and go as I want. Today an undertaker. Tomorrow who
knows. Envy me. I have it better than you. Blind rhetoric is the
only salvation for a thinking man's spirit. I'm off.
[*Lights his cigar. Starts off. Stops. Opens his mouth to speak*]
No. Enough. I'm off. [*Pushes the corpse off*]

[*Blackout*]

# Part 1, Scene 8

HENRY. **HENRY** *is a short, balding man in his late fifties. He is holding a large manuscript at his side. Near him is a chair and a cafe table with a checkered tablecloth. We think he might be giving a speech. But we're not sure because we can't hear him. He mumbles, mutters, coughs, spits — and every once in awhile pounds his manuscript or stamps his foot. Eventually he turns his back on us. Blows his nose. Turns around. Lifts his manuscript above his head — pounds it with his free hand. Sneezes violently. Is taken by a severe stomach cramp — buckles over. Falls into his chair. Recovers.*

HENRY  To continue. [*Sneeze*] To continue from where. [*Sneeze*] As I was ...

[*Coughs. Mumbles. Pulls at his hair. The* **SERVANT** *enters. Hands* **HENRY** *a glass of water. The* **SERVANT** *is dressed as he was — with the addition of a fairly large bow tie*]

Thanks.

SERVANT  I have been asked to tell you that you cannot be heard in the upper balcony.

HENRY  I have no interest in being heard in the upper balcony. Sincere people sit on the ground floor.

SERVANT  But there are gentlemen up there who arrived late.

HENRY  [*standing*] Then let them eat cake!

SERVANT  Sir?

HENRY  Never mind. Got a Kleenex?

SERVANT  But these gentlemen in the upper balcony are from the Pulitzer Committee.

HENRY  Pulitzer. Are you sure. Pulitzer. Go get me a Kleenex. My nose is running.

[**SERVANT** *shrugs. Leaves.* **HENRY** *runs his sleeve under his nose. Raises his head. Speaks in a resounding voice*]

Literature! [*Glances toward balcony*] Literature. The demon rum of educated man. A topic which has defied exploration ever since Voltaire set up logical contradiction as a way of life. The question then is: Am I qualified to contradict Voltaire? [*More restrained. Pause*] Let me begin by telling you something that few of you know. I'm a literary reincarnate. Three lives. The first, John Donne, the second, Herman Melville. The third, I myself, yours truly. [*Gestures ingratiatingly*] Now I know that you have your doubts about me. Some have called me a dirty book writer with pretensions to art and an obsession with blow jobs. And one critic actually accused me of trying to sodomize the Holy Ghost. Astute observations. [*Sneezes*] However, all the shortcomings in my early works can be traced to an unsatisfactory marriage. Divorce, alimony and slander have since solved that problem. [*Pause*] The mystic in Corfu who told me that I had been John Donne and Herman Melville also told me that I, myself, would eventually become an American literary giant. I humbly ask you to endorse that statement. [*Looks around*] Literature! [*Sneezes*] Get me that goddamn Kleenex!!

> [*He sits at the table.* SERVANT *enters. Hands* HENRY *a glass of water and a handkerchief*]

Thanks.

SERVANT     You're welcome. [*Handing* HENRY *a bouquet of flowers*] These are from your ex-wife, sir. She's sitting front row centre. She sends her regards. Reminds you that you are allergic to wool and you should take that jacket off. And also asks that you please stop shouting.

HENRY     [*loud whisper*] Please tell my ex-wife, the morbid bitch, that this is my freelance writer's jacket and it stays on. Tell her that I am free of her idiotic meddling, and that I will shout as loud as I please. Louder, if it will push her any nearer the grave.

SERVANT     Permission as usual to edit your reply, sir? [HENRY *shrugs*] Good. The reply will read — thanks for the flowers — love Henry.

HENRY     Fine. Now get off the stage. No. Wait. Come here.

SERVANT     [*returns.* HENRY *whispers in his ear.* SERVANT *nods. Looks up*] The author wishes to introduce selected readings, and dramatizations from his latest work, *Quiet Days in Limbo*.

> [SERVANT *bows slightly. Leaves.* HENRY *opens manuscript*]

HENRY     Paris. Before the War. Life was crawling along with surly self-confidence. Sleeping. All day. Sexing. All night. Everything was quaint. A cafe where I went to absorb myself with myself. Or chastise myself with still another self. Or listen when I could. To the clatter of artists. And art lovers, and art lovers' lovers. Everyone was half mad with energy, everyone was a bit beautiful. The girls — Gertie, Lillie, Catherine, Gena and the Veronte Sisters from Milan. Fifty francs on a slow night. Dolly cost a little more. She had her own flat over a butcher's shop and she could suck you into the canyon in her bed and make you pray for the end of the world. With Dolly a man could die happy.

> [**DOLLY** *enters. Long, low-cut dress. Ankle bracelets, etc.*
> *Wraps her arms around* **HENRY**'s *neck. Kisses his bald head.*
> **ALADDIN** *enters. Stands at the side.* **DOLLY** *and* **HENRY** *notice*
> *him.* **ALADDIN** *smiles.* **DOLLY** *and* **HENRY** *frown. Look away.*
> *Slightly troubled.* **ALADDIN** *plays a couple of notes on the*
> *pipes.* **DOLLY** *and* **HENRY** *lower their heads.* **ALADDIN**
> *smiles. Leaves. Pause.* **DOLLY** *looks around. Kisses* **HENRY**'s
> *head again.* **HENRY** *looks around. Adjusts himself in his seat*]

DOLLY    Henry.

HENRY    What?

DOLLY    You've been perfuming your scalp again.

HENRY    Pig oil. Helps to preserve the skin.

DOLLY    Where'd you find a pig that smelled like a lilac bush.

HENRY    Barcelona. Spain treats her pigs well. [*Pause*]

DOLLY    Getting just a little fruity in your old age, eh?

HENRY    Maybe I am. Do you want to help me find out for sure.

DOLLY    Let it hang, old man. I've just come to say good-bye.

HENRY    Why?

DOLLY    I'm going home.

HENRY    You go home every morning. What's so special about today that you have to say good-bye.

DOLLY    Home is in Arizona.

HENRY    Arizona disappeared from the face of the earth fifty years ago.

DOLLY    Then I can't think of a safer place to be.

HENRY    Safe? Safe. I haven't heard that word since I left New York.

DOLLY    Well read the newspapers. It's catching up to you.

HENRY    Nonsense. The French won't tolerate it. It was an Englishman who coined the expression — 'better safe than dead.' There's a story about him.

DOLLY    I haven't got time to listen to it.

HENRY    It seems that using that odd rationale unique to the British he took a trip to France during the revolution. He was stoned to death as he left the ship at Calais. They built a monument to him inside a men's lavatory. Opposite the wall reserved for graffiti. There's a bronze plaque at the foot of the monument which the lavatory attendant polishes twice weekly. It reads: In memory of so and so. With the best of both worlds. Safe *and* dead. Have you heard this story before?

DOLLY No.

HENRY Then perhaps I'm lying.

DOLLY Of course you are. That's what you do best.

HENRY Some people will listen to me for hours.

DOLLY Some people have nothing better to do. I've got a train to catch. Now give me a kiss good-bye.

HENRY Is it the Fascists you're afraid of?

DOLLY The Fascists. I've been having nightmares about them. They grab me and take me by force. Make me perform. Force me to do things. Things.

HENRY Be realistic. It's just sex. What could they make you do that you haven't already done.

DOLLY It's one thing to do them voluntarily. You can always blame passion. Or even money. But to be grabbed by the hair with a pistol under your chin and made to crawl around like a puppy is not only frightening but it's undignified. Yeah. Then there'd be no dignity left.

HENRY Dignity. That's another new word isn't it?

DOLLY Yes, it is. And are you saying that I have no right ...

HENRY Oh, you can use it. As a word. But not as an idea. As an idea it just doesn't suit certain classes of people.

DOLLY Name some.

HENRY Politicians, abortionists, actors ... ladies of the gutter.

DOLLY That's why I've never slept with you Henry. You've got a mind like a sewer and a temperament to match. [*She starts off*]

HENRY The Fascists won't touch you. They're men after all, and like all men they're afraid of social disease.

DOLLY Swine. Any diseases I've caught, I've caught from your friends.

HENRY But I have nowhere near two thousand friends.

DOLLY Swine.

HENRY Oh, save your dignity for your new life in Arizona. It's just wasted here.

**DOLLY**  I've got a son, Henry.

**HENRY**  Just one?

**DOLLY**  Just one. He sends me postcards. And he's had his picture in the paper. He uses men like you to dust off his shoes. Little men with perfumed scalps. [*She leaves*]

**HENRY**  [*shouting after her*] Who cares? You could eat shit, get pregnant, catch rabies, or fall off the bloody roof of the Empire State Building. And who the hell would care? [*Pause. Chuckles*] We always argued passionately about absolutely nothing. It was part of an expatriate's charm.

[*Smells flowers. Reads from his manuscript*]
So Dolly went away. She went snarling back to Arizona and her son. The son with pictures in the newspaper ...

Just before the slack-jawed black shirts and the Aryan
butchers with blood on their teeth
came storming out of the woodwork
like cockroaches after the crumbs
Splintering the quiet air where men
Like myself hung comfortably. Before the rush.
Which altered everything. Which was smell or taste
So that fog was smoke and honey, piss

The night was getting thicker
Dolly had gone. Leaving me alone.
With a pain in my groin.
And I recalled the naughty tricks that Gena used to play.
Under the table.
Under everyone's nose.
Playing with my tool ...
And making the table shake.
Wet and delicious.
Naughty. Under the table.
Making me writhe and blush.
Giggling as she worked her tongue
And scratched my thighs.

[**SERVANT** *enters. Carrying the legs of a mannequin. A bit embarrassed.* **HENRY** *gestures for him to leave.* **SERVANT** *remains. Holding the legs like a Shakespearian spear carrier*]

My trousers now around my knees.
Stuck.
While Gena contorted like a love-starved acrobat.
Turning upside down.
My head.
When I was young
And in heat
Getting blown and loved
When I was young in Paris
And believed in the Holy Dove
Assured forever that the power and the mind
Behind the Universe, was love
Was sympathy and love. [*Pause*]
Sympathy and love. [*Closes book. Lowers head. Looks around*]
Before the doubts. The doubts which made me wonder if my
mind had been just slightly damaged. Wondering. A bit to my-
self. A bit to anyone who'd listen. Doubts, dreams, delirium.

> [*Lowers his head. The pipes in the distance. But getting closer
> and louder quickly.* ALADDIN *enters*]

ALADDIN  Mr. Melville. [*No response*] Mr. Melville, let's go back to the
sea.

> [**HENRY** *looks up. Smiles.* **SERVANT** *and* **ALADDIN** *exchange
> smiles*]

[*Blackout*]
[*The pipes. Silence*]

# Part 1, Scene 9

*AHRUN and STEIN stroll on. AHRUN holding an umbrella over STEIN's head.*

AHRUN   Why won't you tell me?

STEIN   What should I tell you.

AHRUN   Just what I want to know.

STEIN   There's knowing. Then there's knowing. There's knowing what you know. And knowing what you want to know. Then there's knowing that you know that you want to know what you say you need to know. I know nothing.

AHRUN   Oh, Stein.

STEIN   People — thinking me wise — have always wanted something from me. They still do. [*Looks away*] Is it wisdom?

AHRUN   Stein!

STEIN   What?

AHRUN   Nothing.

STEIN   Nothing. What do they want of me, that wanting nothing they get less and wanting less, still get nothing ... Oh, I am crippled by my own perception.

AHRUN   I'm sorry for you.

STEIN   Leave me now. You remind me too much of yourself.
        [*Gong. Trumpet.* MITCH *enters. He has the* MASONETTES *in tow. Ropes around all their necks. Burlap bags covering their heads*]

AHRUN   What is this? [MITCH *produces a small leather folder*]

MITCH   My credentials.
        [STEIN *is hiding behind the umbrella.* MITCH *is trying to get a look at her face. They dodge in a very subtle fashion*]

AHRUN   Courier.

MITCH   Diplomatic courier.

AHRUN   Spy?

MITCH   It's a job.

AHRUN   Well, what do you want?

MITCH   Who's this person behind the umbrella.

AHRUN   Never mind.

MITCH   Come on, Madame. Let's have a look at your face.

AHRUN   Now see here. I'm familiar with your tactics.

MITCH   It's just a job. Don't make it any tougher than it already is.

AHRUN   [*to* STEIN] You'd better leave.

MITCH   Just a minute.

AHRUN   Now none of your tricks, you hear. [*To* STEIN] Go ahead.
        [STEIN *leaves.* MITCH *tries to follow, but* AHRUN *blocks the way*]

MITCH   Doesn't matter. I know who she is.

AHRUN   You could be mistaken.

MITCH   We seldom make mistakes.

AHRUN   Arrogant man.

MITCH   Give her back.

AHRUN   No.

MITCH   You'll *have* to give her back.

AHRUN   Is that a threat?

MITCH   No. Of course not. Listen, we know what's going on, you know. The disappearance of − well, let's call them artifacts − museum pieces so to speak.

AHRUN   What do you mean.

MITCH   Museum pieces so to speak.

AHRUN   Yes. You said that.

MITCH   Very important to us. Just disappearing.

AHRUN   Really.

MITCH   All right, let's cut the shit. You just bloody well better give them back.

AHRUN   Don't threaten me.

MITCH   No, of course not. My apologies. [AHRUN *nods*] I'm authorized to offer you a trade. These three young ladies.

AHRUN   For what?

MITCH   Don't be difficult!

AHRUN   Lower your voice.

MITCH   I'm sorry. Listen these people − let's call them cultural titbits − are very important to us.

AHRUN   Why?

MITCH   I'm not authorized to give an answer to that question!

AHRUN   Lower your voice. This is a graveyard.

MITCH   [*looks around curiously*] Look, you can be just as difficult as you want. My government has trained me to handle difficult people so you can just go ahead and be difficult but it ain't, isn't going to help us sort anything out. I order you to give them back.

**AHRUN** No.

**MITCH** I order you to trade them for these girls.

**AHRUN** No.

**MITCH** Damn. [*Pause. Hands* **AHRUN** *the end of the rope which tethers the girls*] Here. You'll have to keep them anyway.

[**AHRUN** *drops the rope. Takes the bags off their heads. The* **MASONETTES** *look around. Curiously. Confused*]

**AHRUN** Why?

**MITCH** Because I can't take them back. No budget for it. One way trip. That's all. Either you keep them or I leave them in the desert.

**AHRUN** All right. They can stay.

**MITCH** Sure. Think of them as a gift from my government.

**AHRUN** Arrogant man.

**MITCH** Now listen, don't be like that. These girls are very valuable in their own way. They represent sort of a class or group. Very unique. Like court jesters. Or dancing bears.

**AHRUN** What do they do?

**MITCH** They're entertainers ... Watch.

[*Immediately. A lively raunchy piece of recorded music. The girls break into a highly polished dance. All smiles and expertise.* **MITCH** *slips out.* **AHRUN** *is enjoying the* **MASONETTES**. *Music and dance stop*]

**AHRUN** [*smiling*] Great leaders are always surrounded by entertainers. British kings. Roman gods. And. American presidents.

[*He snaps his fingers. Music continues*]

[*Blackout*]

## Part 1, Scene 10

AHRUN. SARA *enters. Carrying his robes. But the robes are brighter, more majestic now.*

SARA    Are you ready for these yet.
AHRUN    Just about.
       *[He walks directly downstage. Puts his hands on his hips. Looks around. Pauses. Smiles arrogantly. Returns to Sara]*
       Now. *[She hands him the robes. He begins to put them on over his suit]*

*[Blackout]*

# Part 1, Scene 11

*The* MASONETTES *are in a purple spot. A bit grotesque. The piano player at the piano behind them. They sing* A Blow for Art*. *Then leave. During the song the rest of the cast could be assembling the saloon. The elements: a bar, two tables, six or seven chairs — should be arranged around the piano.* DOC *sits at one of the tables. Plays 'Solitaire'.* STEIN *sits at another table, dressed in cowboy's working clothes. On her head, though, she wears a large black hat with a white feather. She stares silently ahead. (The cock crows. The cock crows again, louder)* DOC *stands. Stretches. Yawns. Stretches. Sits.*

DOC   Whiskey. [*Nothing*] Whiskey.
     [*Nothing. Quickly gathers cards. Stands, throws them over the bar*]
     God it's hot in here ... [*Pause*] Whiskey, you little bastard.
     [*Sits.* HENRY *peeks his head up from behind the bar*]
HENRY   What kind?
DOC   What kind they got?
HENRY   Well, there's this and there's that.
DOC   Which is the best?
HENRY   I don't know.
DOC   Well, when are you gonna find out goddamn it. When?
HENRY   Today, goddamn it, today.
DOC   What's that?
HENRY   Today.
DOC   Well, it's about time, isn't it. Isn't it?
HENRY   Yes, I suppose it is.
DOC   Under normal circumstances, you'd have been dead a month ago.
HENRY   I know.
DOC   You're an idiot, aren't you.
HENRY   Yes, I'm a real jerk.
DOC   Smart ass.
HENRY   [*to himself*] Smart ass yourself.

*Music — Steven Jack, Lyrics — George Walker

DOC      What's that?

HENRY    Do you want a glass for yourself?

DOC      Just bring the bottle. Come on, come on.

         [**HENRY** *grabs a bottle. Rushes around to* **DOC**'*s table.* **DOC**
         *takes the bottle. Drinks. Sighs. Pause*]
         Who are you today?

HENRY    Oh, I'm much better today.

DOC      What's that mean?

HENRY    Means that today I'm myself.

DOC      Just plain Henry?

HENRY    Just plain Henry.

DOC      Sit down.

HENRY    Thanks.

DOC      Who were you yesterday?

HENRY    Weren't you here yesterday?

DOC      No. I was in the tent.

HENRY    The big tent?

DOC      Is there a little tent?

HENRY    I don't know.

DOC      Then that was just another one of your smart ass questions, eh?

HENRY    No. I just wanted to make sure it was the big tent and not some
         other one. I mean that big tent's bad enough, but suppose they've
         got another one or maybe another two, I mean ...

DOC      Shut up.

HENRY    Gladly.

DOC      Now who were you yesterday?

HENRY    I can't remember.

STEIN    [*without turning her head*] He was John Donne. He put his shirt
         on backwards and gave a sermon from the top of the bar.

DOC      Henry, it's a miracle that you've escaped the asylum for so many
         years.

HENRY    Is it?

DOC      All this cow dung about being a — whatyacallit ...

STEIN    Reincarnate. Literary reincarnate.

HENRY    It's not my doing. It's that mystic in Corfu. Corfu. The spring of
         '46. She was a little woman with dirty finger nails and green
         veins under her eyes.

STEIN    [*without turning her head*] Stupid little schizophrenic.

DOC      She mighta told you that you'd been twice before ...

HENRY    Exactly. Born twice before. She said it with a touch of envy.

DOC      But you can't blame her 'cause you think you're three different people all at the same time.

HENRY    Can't I? Do I?

DOC      Three people, Henry. I've seen them all. Yourself and those two other fellas.

HENRY    Pressure.

STEIN    Pressure from what?

HENRY    From being a literary figure.

STEIN    Make one final grasp at your senses man. You're a porno packer. *I'm* a literary figure.

HENRY    Oh, I know Picasso too. [*To* DOC] His friends don't call him Pablo. He once told me that the only reason he painted her portrait was because he'd never had a butch model before.

STEIN    My whip! Where's my whip!

DOC      Sit down, Stein.

STEIN    Eat shit, cowboy.

DOC      Under normal circumstances you'd get a bullet in the head for that.

STEIN    I will not tolerate all of this self-parody.

DOC      Sit down, before you float away.

HENRY    You tell her, Doc.

STEIN    [*sitting*] You tell her, Doc. Kindergarten rhetoric.

HENRY    I know all about you, Stein. You should never have consented to all those biographies. [*To* DOC] She was a teen-age transvestite.

STEIN    [*groans*] Don't need the whip. I'll do it with my bare hands. [*Stands*] Rip flesh. Crush bones. Blood and open wounds.

HENRY    God. [HENRY *backs away.* STEIN *is approaching him with laconic menace.* SARA *enters*]

SARA    Good morning. What's she doing?

DOC      She's hungry.

SARA    Stein.

STEIN    Henry.

         [HENRY *stops suddenly. Stiffens. Heroically. Expands his chest. Bellows*]

HENRY    Cock-a-Doodle-Doo ... Sketch Second ... Two Sides to a Tortoise. [STEIN *stops*] Stand back. And take stock of your odds.

<table>
<tr><td></td><td>Most ugly fearful aspect and horrible shape. Such as Dame Nature selfe ... selfe ... oh.</td></tr>
</table>

STEIN   Selfe mote feare to see.

HENRY   Yes. Thank you.

STEIN   [*to* DOC] It's Herman Melville again.

HENRY   From either or both of two short stories. *Enchanted Isles* and the *Crowing of the Noble Cock.*

SARA   Ah, but Mr. Melville, you never finished *Billy Budd.*

HENRY   That's because I died. You all know the dates, 1819 to 1891. I died after a fruitful and eventful life. My father was a merchant.

DOC   You can forget the life story, Henry.

HENRY   Eat shit, cowboy.

DOC   Under normal circumstances. [*Snaps his fingers*]

SARA   What I was saying, Mr. Melville, was that you were reading to us from *Billy Budd* last time you were here. But you didn't finish.

HENRY   Where was it I left off?

SARA   You were just beginning chapter twenty.

HENRY   Oh yes. You're in for a real treat. Chapter twenty is purple. A marvellous allegory. The entire table of opposites. Good-evil, true-false, being-non-being, life-death, up-down.

[DOC *and* STEIN *are mouthing the table of opposites*]

STEIN   You needed a chapter. I could do it with five lines.

HENRY   In which of the two sexes have you enlisted today? You great mysterious hulk.

[*Music. Oriental procession march. Enter* ALADDIN *and the* SERVANT *casually throwing flowers on the floor. They are followed by* AHRUN. *All three of these men should appear older than they were.* AHRUN *is fully decked out and carrying a walking stick*]

AHRUN   So you've been at it again. Do you deny it?

ALADDIN   They can't. I have been listening at the door.

AHRUN   Tell me later.

ALADDIN   Nothing much to tell. Petty disagreements.

AHRUN   Tell me later. Good morning, daughter.

SARA   Good morning.

AHRUN   You may leave now.

[SARA *shrugs. Starts off.* AHRUN *takes her aside*]

It's good that you mix easily with them. Visit them as often as

|         | you like. Get them to trust you. |
|---------|----------------------------------|
| SARA    | Sure. [SARA *leaves*] |
| AHRUN   | Go with Aladdin to the tent, Henry. |
| HENRY   | To that name I answer nothing. |
| AHRUN   | But that's your name. |
| HENRY   | No it's not. |
| ALADDIN | Your name is Henry, Henry. |
| HENRY   | No. |
| STEIN   | They're right, you know. |
| HENRY   | No they're not. |
| DOC     | Poor ole Henry. |

[HENRY *grabs the bottle from* DOC. *Takes a long drink. He plants his feet apart*]

HENRY You are all bit players in an arrogant farce. And I am the eternal navigator.

[AHRUN *gestures.* ALADDIN *and the* SERVANT *move slightly toward* HENRY. HENRY, *backing up*]

What's this. You can't touch the eternal navigator. He's sublime. He's the whirlpool in the ocean of the mind. Stand back. Natives no can have firewater. [*On tip toes*] There is room in a man for only one passion. Mine is self-pity.

[HENRY *breaks the bottle over the bar. Slashes both his wrists*]

| AHRUN | Why did you do that? |
|-------|----------------------|
| HENRY | I don't know. I think it was a mistake. |

[HENRY *passes out.* ALADDIN *and the* SERVANT *pick him up*]

AHRUN Bandage him. Then take him to the tent.

[ALADDIN *nods. They leave*]

I'm sure he'll be all right.

| DOC   | Who cares. |
|-------|-----------|
| STEIN | Who cares. |
| DOC   | I wanna complain about the whiskey. |
| AHRUN | Go ahead. |
| DOC   | It's lousy. |
| AHRUN | You'll get used to it. |
| DOC   | [*stands*] You're right, I will. [*Sits*] |
| AHRUN | Fine. |
| DOC   | I wanna complain about the deck of cards. |
| AHRUN | What's wrong with it? |

DOC    There's no Ace of Clubs.

AHRUN    Is that all?

DOC    Whatya mean — is that all — Jesus, don't you know nothing? I play solitaire. I gotta play solitaire 'cause none of these namby pambies will play poker with me.

AHRUN    That's unfortunate, isn't it?

DOC    Yeah. Unfortunate. 'Cause you can't play solitaire without the Ace of Clubs.

AHRUN    You'll think of something.

DOC    [*stands*] You're right. I will. [*Sits*]

AHRUN    Anything else?

STEIN    Where's my whip?

AHRUN    You don't have a whip.

STEIN    I'm a stage-coach driver, aren't I?

AHRUN    I don't know. Are you?

STEIN    Bringing me into a saloon. I had to be something, eh? When in Rome, eh? I wasn't going to be a bar girl. Now where's my bloody whip?

AHRUN    I've told you. You do not have a whip.

AHRUN    Then get me one. I will not be incomplete. It's nerve wracking. Christ. Couldn't you have made it a hotel lobby. I've got a trunk full of tweed suits. You know a hotel lobby's just as American as a saloon, don't you? Eh?

AHRUN    I'm sorry. A saloon was the first thing to come to mind.

STEIN    Mechanical thinking, cliches. You know that, don't you. It's a stupid cliche.

AHRUN    Perhaps.

DOC    I like it just fine.

STEIN    You eat straw. What advice could you give to the chef at the Ritz?

DOC    What's that mean?

STEIN    Bubble gum. Donkey brains.

AHRUN    Stein.

STEIN    All right. No more arguments. Arguments are just food for the intellectually starved. It's a saloon and a saloon it stays. Saloon, saloon, no better no worse. Some say, some who stay and those who don't, don't. Don't say or stay.

DOC    Will you shut her up.

| | |
|---|---|
| AHRUN | Stein, please. |
| STEIN | I will not be incomplete. A stage-coach driver needs a whip. |
| DOC | She wants it to bully Henry. |
| STEIN | I want it to beat the goddamn horses on the ass, cowboy. |
| DOC | How come you don't play cards, Stein? |
| STEIN | I do. I play canasta. [*To* AHRUN] Will you get me a whip? |
| AHRUN | I have to think about it. |
| DOC | What's canasta? |
| STEIN | A game. |
| DOC | So teach me. And we'll play. |
| STEIN | Just the two of us. |
| DOC | Yeah. Just the two of us. |
| STEIN | Ah. How sweet. And when shall we play? Just the two of us? |
| DOC | When things get slow. |
| STEIN | Oh, when things get slow. |
| AHRUN | Why, Stein? Why? |
| STEIN | If things got any slower we'd all be experiencing perpetual deja vu. |
| DOC | What? Listen, you know I don't understand French. So talk English or don't talk at all. |
| STEIN | Cretin! |
| AHRUN | Please. |
| DOC | Nobody talks like that to Doc Halliday and lives for long. |
| STEIN | How is it that every time you open your mouth you satirize yourself. |
| AHRUN | Please. |
| DOC | You should talk. |
| AHRUN | Be quiet! |
| STEIN | Ah. |
| DOC | Ah. [STEIN *and* DOC *both take their seats.* AHRUN *composes himself*] |
| AHRUN | Why are you always arguing about the pettiest of things? |
| STEIN | None of your business. |
| STEIN | That's right. |
| AHRUN | I haven't heard any of you ask why you've been brought here. Or what's going to be done with you. Or how long you're going to stay. Why? |
| DOC | None of your business. |

STEIN   That's right.
AHRUN   But don't any of you feel strange at not being where you should be. Or with who you want to be with.
DOC   Where should we be?
STEIN   Who do we want to be with?
AHRUN   Well, I'm not sure.
STEIN   No. It's quite a problem isn't it?
AHRUN   But I have theories.
STEIN   Theories?
AHRUN   Theories.
STEIN   Poor old man.
AHRUN   And a few beliefs.
DOC   Beliefs, eh?
STEIN   Poor old man.
AHRUN   Am I?
STEIN   It seems so.
AHRUN   Yes ... Yes ... [*His head lowered. He starts off*]
STEIN   Yes, that's a good fellow ... Go away and lie down. Leave us alone.
AHRUN   Yes. [*Walking off. Stops. Suddenly turns around*] Fame is a fickle commodity. Not bad, mind you. Just fickle.
DOC   So what?
STEIN   Exactly.
AHRUN   It needs to be guided, so to speak. And if it's guided in the right direction, it can create things. Purpose. Glamour. Mystique. [*Pause*] Artists. Or folk heroes. All things which we find very scarce around here.
STEIN   What happens then?
AHRUN   Folk-lore.
STEIN   And then?
AHRUN   More folk-lore.
STEIN   And then?
AHRUN   And then ... and you can − and then there's always ...
STEIN   Yes?
DOC   What?
         [AHRUN *shakes his head violently. Turns. Leaves. Pause.* DOC *is cleaning his finger nails.* STEIN *is staring off*]
STEIN   Do you know where we are?

DOC   No.
STEIN   Do you care?
DOC   No. Do you?
STEIN   Not in the least.
DOC   Do you want to leave?
STEIN   Of course not. Do you?
DOC   I'm not sure.
STEIN   Do you have any place to go?
DOC   Maybe. No, I don't. [*Pause*]
STEIN   Why can't you go home?
DOC   A lot of people back there think I'm a fraud.
STEIN   Are you?
DOC   Don't know. [*Pause*] How old are you?
STEIN   Ladies.
DOC   What?
STEIN   Ladies don't answer questions like that. [*Pause*]
DOC   Teach me how to play canasta?
STEIN   Maybe. [*Turn to each other. Shrug. Stare off*]

[*Blackout*]


END OF PART I

# Part 2, Scene 12

*The following is in darkness. Trumpet call. Traditional. Again.*
*Discordant. Lights up.*
**AHRUN** *at the bar. Flipping through his sketch pad. Showing the*
*drawings to the* **SERVANT** *who is standing behind the bar.*
*Serving. At the other end of the bar, watching them is* **MITCH.**
*Dressed as an Arab. His tongue hanging from his mouth.* **AHRUN**
*is drinking heavily. Pointing to the sketch pad.*

| | |
|---|---|
| AHRUN | Classical heroes. Lear, Othello, Prospero. |
| SERVANT | Ambitious men. |
| AHRUN | Heroes! Classical artists. Rubens, Renoir ... |
| SERVANT | Talented men. |
| AHRUN | Famous men! |
| SERVANT | Ambitious men. |
| AHRUN | Fame is the artist's only excuse for existence. And fame is every man's right. That's logic. |
| SERVANT | Poorly constructed. |
| AHRUN | Logic! |
| SERVANT | And the Americans? |
| AHRUN | They're concerned only with being legendary. |
| SERVANT | Perhaps. |
| AHRUN | Perhaps not? |
| SERVANT | Yes. [*Pause*] |
| AHRUN | Legends. Mystery. Style. The passing of time. [*Pause*] I still have visions. But now I find that I also have arthritis. Theories. Myths. Men. Mad men. Mad women. Cowboys. |
| SERVANT | Are we getting any younger? |
| AHRUN | Speculation. Conjecture. Give up before it drives you mad. [*To* SERVANT] What do you say? |
| SERVANT | What can I say? |

> [**AHRUN** *grabs the bottle from the* **SERVANT.** *Hides it under*
> *hip robes. Leaves.* **SERVANT** *watches him go. Then looks at*
> **MITCH. SERVANT** *tries to slide* **MITCH** *a drink along the bar.*
> *The glass won't slide. So the* **SERVANT** *gives up. Drinks it*
> *himself*]

MITCH [*over his shoulder*] Will you be bribed?

SERVANT A bribe is a dangerous thing.

MITCH Not necessarily.

SERVANT Speaking historically.

MITCH But speaking practically ...

SERVANT Speaking historically is more important to me.

MITCH Relax. And let me reward your soul.

SERVANT We should leave my soul out of it. History has been unkind to traitors. Literature also treats them with very little respect.

MITCH I'm authorized to offer you the governorship of the State of Indiana.

SERVANT I accept. What must I do.

MITCH [*MITCH rolls him a small bottle of pills*] Keep everyone drugged. [*STEIN and SARA enter. STEIN seats SARA at a chair. Goes behind her. Begins to comb SARA's hair. MITCH nods at the SERVANT. SERVANT pours two glasses of wine. Places them on a tray. Puts pills into both glasses. MITCH takes a telegram from his pocket. Goes over to STEIN*] Telegram for you. [*STEIN takes it. Reads*] Any answer?

STEIN Yes. Write it down.

MITCH [*produces pencil and paper*] Go ahead.

STEIN I have long since stopped returning to America for my relatives' funerals. I am only moved now by conscience. And conscience is only moved by responsibility. I am not responsible for my brother's death. Ergo I remain. My position my name my reputation are such that I need never move again. I have finally become guiltless in my own eyes. Stop.

MITCH I thought as much.

STEIN What?

MITCH Nothing.

STEIN Send it.

MITCH Of course.
[*MITCH goes back to corpse. Starts to push it off. Nods at SERVANT. Leaves. SERVANT takes STEIN and SARA their drinks. They both swallow them immediately. Put glasses on tray. SERVANT returns to the bar. STEIN continues to comb SARA's hair. Pause*]

STEIN I've sat for portraits for two men of genius. Both of them asked me to turn my chin slightly into the sun. Both of them remarked that my sullenness was most attractive at midday. It's true that the glow of the sun can enhance a person's gloom. But I've always felt that late evening was my best time. Others agree. It was said that at night I could fill any room with anticipation just by raising my hand to my lips. A yawn correctly placed can be as devastating as a ton of dynamite. The manipulation of boredom was one of my fortes. I have never experienced the extremities of love and hate. My emotions have survived in a neutrality of sincere indifference. For my country — which I left when I was young and returned to when I was younger still, I feel nothing except an obligation to confuse its citizens. By being both progressively obscure and traditionally literate. I have never been an American. I have never been a Parisienne. Likewise I have never been a Jew nor a woman nor a human being. Always I have been — an artist.

SARA    I love you, Stein.

STEIN    Small bones. Narrow neck. Tiny breasts.

SARA    I'm sorry.

STEIN    Just an observation. It doesn't mean anything one way or the other. What did you say before?

SARA    I said — I love you, Stein.

STEIN    I don't ask much any more. Not because I don't want anything but because I have no place to put anything. After all this time, I find that I am homeless.

SARA    What's it like to be famous?

STEIN    What's it like outside?

SARA    Hot.

STEIN    I don't care. Do up your dress. Everyone will see your breasts.

SARA    It's not undone.

STEIN    I'm going for a walk.

     [*As she is leaving she meets* DOC *who is just coming in*]

     Tell me what it's like outside. And don't lie. You hear?

DOC    There's a desert. Lots of sand. And the odd fig tree.

STEIN    I know that. Is it day or is it night?

DOC    Day.

STEIN    Thanks. [*Leaves*]

SARA    What's wrong with her?

DOC    She was sitting out in the sun yesterday. Trying to get the old man to paint her portrait. I think she might have got sunstroke.
       [DOC *sits. Opens up a book which he has carried in. Starts mouthing muted sounds. He went, she went, they went, etc*]

SARA   What are you reading?
       [*No response. She moves to* DOC's *table. Points at the book*]
       May I? [DOC *shrugs*] Primary reader.

DOC    Yeah.

SARA   Primary reader!

DOC    Yeah, yeah. Primary reader. Go shout it to everyone, why don't ya.

SARA   Can't you read?

DOC    Sure I can read. That's what I was just doing. Reading.

SARA   But you're still learning — is that right?

DOC    Maybe.

SARA   Either you can read or you can't.

DOC    Look, there are some things I can read and some things I have to learn to read. It's all a matter of whatyacallit. The gradual. No the relative. Yeah. It's all a matter of the relative.

SARA   How about that.

DOC    I've never been surrounded by so many wise asses before. This book, that book, I've read this, what have you read wise ass.
       [*Grabs the book*] I'll learn in my own good time.

SARA   But you must know how to read. You're a doctor.

DOC    The hell I am.

SARA   A dentist. You're a dentist.

DOC    No. That's a lie.

SARA   I read somewhere that ...

DOC    I tell you it's a lie.

SARA   So why'd they call you Doc?

DOC    I forget.

SARA   You're lying.

DOC    How'd you like a slap in the mouth, pest.

SARA   Why!!

DOC    I delivered whores' babies. When things slowed down at the poker table, I made money by helping a midwife in a cat house. It got me a nickname and it stuck.

SARA   That's a lie.

DOC   No. Everything else is a lie. That's the truth.

SARA   You were a marshal. That's not a lie.

DOC   Never been a marshal.

SARA   Some kind of peace officer.

DOC   No.

SARA   Then what were you.

DOC   I forget. [*Pause*] Where was it again that you heard I was a marshal?

SARA   I read it.

DOC   It's gotta be a lie.

SARA   And you killing all those outlaws. That's a lie too, eh?

DOC   Why are you asking me all these questions?

SARA   [*firmly*] Is it a lie?

DOC   Well, I don't know if they were all outlaws. Don't even know if any of them were outlaws.

> [SERVANT *brings* DOC *a glass of whiskey.* DOC *guzzles it. But he is suspicious.* SERVANT *returns to bar*]

SARA   Did you kill many men?

DOC   A few.

SARA   Why?

DOC   Different reasons.

SARA   Give one.

DOC   I liked it.

SARA   I don't believe you.

> [*She stands. Pause.* DOC *is looking her over*]

DOC   I've got a hard on.

SARA   It's impossible. You couldn't like it.

DOC   Do you wanna kiss me? Do you wanna sit on my lap?

SARA   It's easier to kill yourself than it is to kill someone else.

DOC   Hey, what've you got on underneath your dress?

SARA   Was it easy?

> [*Pause. He grabs her. Sits her on his lap. Is undoing her dress during this speech*]

DOC   [*totally preoccupied*] Easy. Like killing yourself. As easy as that. The first was the easiest because I wanted to kill myself real bad about then.

SARA   Why?

DOC   He said something. Can't remember what. And I shot him.

SARA  What did it feel like?

DOC  I wanted to kill myself, but I killed him instead. Big deal. Same thing. No feeling one way or the other.

SARA  That's awful

DOC  Oh, it's not so bad. [*Kisses her neck*] About two months later I killed two men at the same time. Now that I think, I enjoyed a bit. Good for the balls.

[*Puts her hand on his crotch*]

SARA  Let me go.

DOC  [*holding onto her*] Shot them in a bath-house. One of them was in the tub. The other one was brushing his hair.

SARA  Defenceless?

DOC  Naked as those whores' babies. [*Pause*] They both had kinda dirty blonde hair.

SARA  So what?

DOC  Can't stand that kind of hair. Don't like hair that isn't one solid colour. Black, brown, red, white. Nothing in between.

SARA  You can't mean that you killed them because you didn't like the colour of their hair.

DOC  What did it say in the books?

SARA  About what?

DOC  About why I shot those fellas in the bath house.

SARA  Nothing. [*He strokes her breasts. Her neck*]

DOC  Do you want me to undress you?

SARA  No. Yes. No.

[*He kisses her. She does not resist.* SARA *says softly*]

You've killed defenceless men. [DOC *smiles*] You're a murderer.

DOC  [*kisses her*] You like it, don't you?

SARA  No, of course, I don't like it. You're a ...

DOC  Yeah. [*Kisses her*] It doesn't matter though, does it. 'Cause I'm still whatyacallit. Just like the rest of them. Whatyacallit? Eternal?

SARA  You mean immortal.

DOC  Yeah.

SARA  [*softly*] Animal.

[*She puts her arms around his neck. Kisses him. They hold. Long pause.* DOLLY *enters. She is dressed like a saloon girl. Carrying a suitcase and a large scrap book*]

DOLLY  [*to* SERVANT] Give me a drink, Sahib. [SERVANT *does so*] Here's
       to the both of you ... Hey!
          [*Pounding on the bar.* DOC *and* SARA *look up*]
       Hi ... Come on! Say hello.
DOC    Hello.
DOLLY  That a boy. Now you little girl. Say hello.
SARA   Hello.
DOLLY  Good. Sweet girl. Pleasant cordialities. Now get your ass off my
       man's lap. No, I take that back. Stay where you are. You look
       enchanting right where you are. Innocent — and — what are you,
       Doc? If she's innocence, what are you?
DOC    Experience?
DOLLY  Good boy.
SARA   Who are you?
DOLLY  Tell her.
DOC    Her name's Dolly.
DOLLY  [*approaching them*] Good boy. Good girl.
SARA   Glad to meet you.
DOLLY  [*patting* SARA *on the head*] Little darling. Sweet child. Do your
       dress up, honey. You shouldn't give him too much too soon.
       He'll lose track of protocol and have you doing obscene things
       before he even knows your last name.
DOC    It's none of your business, Dolly.
DOLLY  Be quiet, John. I'm talking to your tart. Sorry honey. I take that
       back.
SARA   What's she talking about.
DOC    She's out of her mind.
DOLLY  Oh, John, you flatterer you. You'd better put yourself together
       little girl. Your father's coming.
          [SARA *stands. Adjusts her clothes.* DOLLY *pats* DOC *on the
          head. Produces a knife from somewhere. Puts knife under*
          DOC's *chin. Grabs his hair. Yanks his head back*]
SERVANT  I can't watch this.
          [*He takes a large bottle of liquor, the pills and leaves*]
DOLLY  I've been having nightmares, John. I slit open your jugular vein.
       But you don't die.
SARA   Don't hurt him.
DOC    Don't watch.

DOLLY   So brave. How come so brave with a knife at your neck, John?
DOC   It's just blood.
DOLLY   Yes. In these nightmares the blood is pouring out of your neck.
And you just sit there with a silly smirk on your face. Are you
smirking, John?
DOC   Yeah.
DOLLY   I used to worry that I wouldn't be able to find you. Stopped
worrying about that when I started to believe that I'd find you by
accident. Trip over a stone and see you eating dirt with all the
other maggots.
DOC   Same old Dolly.
DOLLY   Go on vacation. Walk down an unfamiliar street. Answer an ad
for a bar girl or a girl who can sing a song. Let your mind
casually pick up the odd rumour. You'll find him.
SARA   Please don't hurt him.
DOC   Turn your head away.
DOLLY   And now he seems so brave with that knife under his chin. And
then there's that arrogant smirk. I could never understand it.
Because I remember how, when I first met you, you were afraid
of the dark. And any sound a bit like a gun being cocked would
make you throw up. But that was years ago. And look, I haven't
aged at all. And I knew you hadn't either. I heard that you'd been
killed in Kansas. I mourned. And while I was mourning I heard
you'd been killed in New Mexico and Wyoming. I stopped
mourning. But I kept hearing about you dying at different places
at different times. Tucson, Cheyenne. As far away as Sac-
ramento. It was very confusing. Then I started looking in the
mirror. Long hard looks. There wasn't a single line in my face
and none came. My breasts didn't sag. My shoulders didn't
slope. I stayed the same. Just the way I was when that reporter
from New York took our picture in Dodge City. Doc Halliday and
his mistress Dolly Stulletto. The only time I've ever had my
name in a newspaper, and they spelled it wrong. [Pause] So then I
understood. Many look like they're making it, but only a few,
and not necessarily the best of them, really do. [Pause] Just for
kicks, darling. I know you'll understand.
      [She runs the knife along his neck]
SARA   He's bleeding.

DOLLY   Uh-huh. [DOC *takes out handkerchief. Runs it along his neck*]

DOC   Just a drop. [HENRY *runs in. Perspiring. Frantic. His wrists are bandaged*]

HENRY   They want my mind. My mind belongs to Jesus.
[ALADDIN *and* SERVANT *can be seen crossing at the back. The* SERVANT *is holding a glass of liquor*]

SARA   Reverend Donne?

HENRY   Aye. Yes. They want my mind, you know. And my mind belongs to Jesus. Master create a diversion.
[*He hides behind the bar.* ALADDIN *and the* SERVANT *come on.* ALADDIN *poorly dressed as a cowboy. Carrying a toy gun*]

ALADDIN   Where is he?

SARA   Who?

ALADDIN   We're not getting anywhere. He saw all those electric wires and he went berserk. [*To* SERVANT] Look outside.
[SERVANT *starts off. Decides to check behind bar. Gets there. Looks down. Obviously having found* HENRY. *Mixes a drink with several pills. Bends and disappears behind the bar with the drink*]

SARA   Why are you dressed like that. [ALADDIN *examines himself*]

ALADDIN   I don't know.

SARA   You look silly.

ALADDIN   I do? [*Sighs*] We're not getting anywhere. [*To* DOC] Why won't you co-operate. It's the decent thing to do.

DOC   I don't know what you're talking about.

ALADDIN   You all say that. Stein sits out in the sun all day like a gopher. She goes a bit mad. But she doesn't die. Well, I've decided that that's just the way things are. A peculiar but obvious fact. What really bothers me is the fact that she doesn't wonder why she doesn't die.

DOC   She just doesn't. Why wonder?

ALADDIN   Because you have to wonder, you horrible brute. It's natural to wonder.

DOC   Maybe.

ALADDIN   Don't say maybe any more. Don't say you don't know, you don't care, you ain't got a clue, or so help me ...

DOC   [*stands*] What?!

ALADDIN   Why won't you co-operate?

| | |
|---|---|
| **DOC** | What do you want? |
| **SARA** | He can't tell you. |
| **ALADDIN** | I can. I've thought it over. I can tell you. |
| **SARA** | Then go ahead. |
| **ALADDIN** | Yes! Yes. |
| **SARA** | Nonsense. What do you want from all your nonsense? |
| **ALADDIN** | Mystery. [*Pause*] The O.K. Corral. The Texas Rangers, Paul Revere, Donald Duck, Jessie Owens, Annie Oakley, Betty Crocker, Buster Keaton, Robert E. Lee, Aunt Jemima, George Washington, George Washington Carver, the Wright Brothers, Charles Lindberg, those men on the moon and what's go grand about the Grand Canyon? |
| **SARA** | You're obsessed. |
| **ALADDIN** | I'm passionate! |
| **HENRY** | [*Standing up. His hair is now white*] I'm getting old. My name is Henry. You can have my mystery because it's cheap. I missed the boat. I'm losing my hair. They'll say he wrote five books, none of which won a Pulitzer Prize, and they'll spread my ashes over a parking lot. I'm not one of them. Something went wrong ... A toast to old age. |
| **ALL** | SKOL!!! |

[*Blackout*]

## Part 2, Scene 13

AHRUN. *In the desert. Drinking. Muttering. Flipping through his sketch pad. Holding his paint brush.*

AHRUN    Surround yourself with familiar things because the world is conspiring to deprive you of your senses.
    *[Takes a long drink.* ALADDIN *comes on. Carrying his lamp and a small rolled-up carpet]*

ALADDIN    I'm sorry. *[Starts off]*

AHRUN    For what.

ALADDIN    In such a large desert a man should be able to die alone.

AHRUN    Have you come out here to die.

ALADDIN    Of course. Haven't you?

AHRUN    No. The thought of giving up is repulsive to me.

ALADDIN    Strange. But I find it comforting. Do you understand that?

AHRUN    No. *[Starts off]*

ALADDIN    You're forgetting something.

AHRUN    What?

ALADDIN    Good-bye.
    *[*AHRUN *nods. Leaves.* ALADDIN *sits down. Cross-legged. Lowers his head.* MITCH *and* SERVANT *come on. Stop some distance from* ALADDIN. MITCH *is disguised as Lawrence of Arabia. The* SERVANT *is carrying a glass full of liquor]*

MITCH    Have you put the pills in that drink?

SERVANT    Yes.

MITCH    Then go give it to him.

SERVANT    Yes. *[*SERVANT *walks over to* ALADDIN. *Looks. Bends down. Looks at* ALADDIN*'s face. Stands. Returns to* MITCH] I can't.

MITCH    Why not?

SERVANT    He's beaten.

MITCH    Is he breathing?

SERVANT    Barely.

MITCH    Then he's not beaten. Give him the drink.

SERVANT    I quit

MITCH    Why?

SERVANT    Conscience. *[He leaves]*

MITCH  Conscience.

[MITCH *walks over to* ALADDIN. *Sits cross-legged next to him*]

Look up. [*No response*] Look up. I'm back.

ALADDIN  Who?

MITCH  Lawrence.

ALADDIN  I've seen a picture of Lawrence. He was shorter.

MITCH  I was shorter. I'm taller now.

ALADDIN  Go away.

MITCH  I'm back. I need your help.

ALADDIN  Go away.

MITCH  Get up. Remember Damascus.

ALADDIN  Leave me alone.

MITCH  Death to the Turks. The best of you brings me the most Turkish dead.

ALADDIN  Lawrence was British.

MITCH  In the desert, no one can afford to be British.

ALADDIN  Listen, I just want to be left alone.

MITCH  Return the Americans to America. [*Pause*]

ALADDIN  If you were Lawrence, you'd do me a favour.

MITCH  A favour for a favour.

ALADDIN  [*handing his gun to* MITCH] Shoot me.

MITCH  Help me get rid of the Americans.

ALADDIN  A favour for a favour?

MITCH  As always.

ALADDIN  Right. You first. Shoot.

MITCH  And then how could you help me?

ALADDIN  Lawrence would think of a way. [*Pause*]

MITCH  Remember Damascus!

ALADDIN  Go away.

[MITCH *is looking curiously at* ALADDIN. ALADDIN *is staring off*]

[*Blackout*]

## Part 2, Scene 14

*The tent.* AHRUN *is painting* STEIN's *portrait.*

STEIN      Your daughter is pregnant.

AHRUN    I know.

STEIN      Do you know who the father is?

AHRUN    I believe so.

STEIN      It's the cowboy.

AHRUN    Mr. Halliday. Yes. At first I was unhappy. But then it occurred to me that a grandchild of this sort might be very unique. Heredity, like certain other things, is very puzzling. Almost anything can happen. Certain things get transferred, passed on ... Please lift your chin.

STEIN      Be sure to set the eyes deeply in the head. It gives the face a prophetic look.

AHRUN    It will just make you look tired.

STEIN      Same thing.

AHRUN    No it's not.

STEIN      Yes it is! [*Pause*]

AHRUN    You once told me that before you came here you had never heard of me. Do you still say that.

STEIN      Yes.

AHRUN    Am I not a king. Am I not an artist. [*Pause*] Listen, I've sold my paintings to people from all over the world.

STEIN      You're still nobody where I come from.

AHRUN    That's very discouraging.

STEIN      Just keep plugging away.

AHRUN    I don't have much time left.

STEIN      Perhaps you'll be discovered.

AHRUN    Why don't you discover me?

STEIN      I discover genius. Anything less I leave to fate.

AHRUN    That's understandable, of course.

STEIN      Perhaps you should die.

AHRUN    I will.

STEIN      But there is death and there is death.

AHRUN    I don't understand.

STEIN      Of course not. Because the subject of death is taboo, you see.

The last real taboo. The last frontier of ignorance. Therefore, it has its own mythology. Anything goes, so to speak.

AHRUN   Please continue. I like to hear you talk.

STEIN   Yes. So many people have said that to me. I like to talk. It — anyway, there is death by passivity and death by aggression. One the end as man understands it. The other the beginning as man doesn't even begin to understand it. Where the end ceases to be the end and instead becomes the beginning. And more. The beginning of a long line of other beginnings. Rose is a rose is a rose is a rose, and so on ... That was a rather clever joke. If you'd been clever you would have laughed.

AHRUN   Sorry. I was thinking. Of beginnings and endings and aggressions. I was — what are you after, Stein? A cheap game of pleasure. To confuse me. To belittle me ...

STEIN   To continue. Death cannot be allowed to come freely to you. You must go to it. Use it. Manipulate it. Then move on from there.

AHRUN   I'm sorry. No I'm not sorry. Yes, I'm ...

STEIN   Have you heard of the eternal harmonies of music ... Why should man be less than music?

AHRUN   Perhaps he shouldn't.

STEIN   Some of it is in the name. The title. If you were called the *Hungarian Rhapsody* you would be in the minds of countless millions.

AHRUN   The *Hungarian Rhapsody??*

STEIN   The flexibility of laws. I say time can run backwards. The legend can precede the fact. Follow?

AHRUN   No.

STEIN   Go to death. Be aggressive. Presume that you are famous. Let the world prove you wrong. Things will begin from there. Rot and return. Rot and return. Rot and return. *[Mumbles]*

AHRUN   *[nodding, nodding. Pause]* No I do not follow you, Stein!

STEIN   Well that's too bad, isn't it?

      *[*ALADDIN *enters carrying a box with electric wires attached to it. He is pale. Eyes slightly vacant looking]*

ALADDIN   May I attach the wires to your head?

STEIN   Sure. *[*ALADDIN *proceeds to do so]* You know I'm fond of abuse.

ALADDIN   Don't confuse me, Stein.

STEIN   Anyway, what more can you take. I've just told him everything about everything.

ALADDIN   Is that true? [AHRUN *shakes his head.* ALADDIN *to* STEIN] Open your mouth please.

STEIN   Realizing that by everything, I actually mean 'mathematics.' And that all I say can be substantiated by referring to the nineteenth proposition of the seventh book of Euclid.

ALADDIN   [STEIN *opens her mouth.* ALADDIN *inserts a metal disc*] Please bite the metal. Thank you.

[ALADDIN *throws a switch on the machine.* STEIN *stiffens — body — fingers, etc. Throws her head back as if electrocuted*]

AHRUN   She's quite mad, you know. She could go on for hours and never make a bit of sense. You don't look well.

ALADDIN   I'm dead.

AHRUN   Oh. [*Pause*] I will not give up. We must be patient. I'm going to have a grandchild. A very special child.

[*Turns toward* STEIN]

She's really quite mad, you know.

[*Blackout*]

# Part 2, Scene 15

MITCH. *A caddy. Standing. Wearing sunglasses. Whistling.*
*Grey-haired. Rocking back and forth on his heels. Over his*
*shoulder a golf bag full of golf clubs. He tosses a golf ball into the*
*air aimlessly. Looking occasionally over his shoulder. The*
SERVANT *enters. He is pushing the covered corpse on a table. He*
*appears older.* MITCH *now uses a thick American accent.*

MITCH     Hi there!

SERVANT     Yes.

MITCH     How's things?

SERVANT     I beg your pardon.

MITCH     How are ya?

SERVANT     I am fine. How are you?

MITCH     The baby's ass, kid. A little hot, but mostly peaches and cream.

SERVANT     Are you lost?

MITCH     Not in a million, buddy. Never been lost in my life.

SERVANT     Do you know where you're going?

MITCH     Uh-huh. Straight ahead.

SERVANT     Oh. Me too. I'll show you the way if you want.

MITCH     Okay. But I gotta wait for my boss.

SERVANT     Your boss?

MITCH     Yeah. He's down in the bunker taking a leak.

SERVANT     Bunker?

MITCH     Oh. That sand hole. Over there. He'll just be a sec.

SERVANT     What's that on your shoulders?

MITCH     Spalding 900's. Everyone of them hand-fitted for the boss.
Peaches and cream. Two thousand bucks.

SERVANT     Oh.

MITCH     Hey boss! We got ourselves a guide! He'll just be a sec. He's in a
hurry to get there. I don't know where 'there' is — 'cause he don't
tell me nothin' except which iron he wants on a narrow fairway.
But I know he's in a hurry 'cause we've passed at least fifty
courses and he ain't so much as turned an eye. Straight ahead,
Mitch. He says. So straight ahead we go.

SERVANT     I see.

MITCH     Here he comes now.

SERVANT   Where?

MITCH   [*pointing*] There.

[**SERVANT** *looks. Strains. Puts on his glasses. Looks again. Stiffens. Screams. Hobbles off as quickly as he can.* **MITCH** *walks downstage. Laughs*]

One transition after another. I'm amazed by my versatility. We're right behind you, old timer.

[*Wheels the corpse's table off*]

[*Blackout*]

# Part 2, Scene 16

*The* **SALOON**. **STEIN** *sits motionless staring off.* **DOC** *is looking down the barrel of his gun.* **DOLLY** *is flipping through a photograph album.* **HENRY** *is in a rocking chair on top of the bar. Rocking back and forth. Drinking from a bottle — which he keeps in his lap. A cane in one hand.*

DOLLY    There I am in Kansas City, 1860.

DOC    That was a good year. Even in Kansas City.

DOLLY    God. Look at the lines on that dress. Classic. You bought me that dress, Doc.

DOC    Did I?

DOLLY    Brought it into my room one night. Threw it down on the bed and said — put it on and never take it off.

DOC    I see you took it off.

DOLLY    There I am with my sister. Do you remember my sister, John?

DOC    No.

DOLLY    Grace. Red hair. Big bones.

DOC    Knew a lot of women with big bones.

DOLLY    You seduced her.

DOC    She seduced me.

DOLLY    Thought you didn't remember her?

DOC    Don't. Just remember being seduced.

DOLLY    1905.

DOC    Another good year.

DOLLY    Midsummer.

DOC    Uh-huh.

DOLLY    The twenty-third of July. [DOC *nods*] My birthday.

DOC    Really.

DOLLY    You rotten son-of-a-bitch.

DOC    Watch your mouth. [*Pause*]

DOLLY    Here I am outside Claire's Cafe, 1938. Paris.

HENRY    Paris?

DOLLY    Do you remember Paris, Henry?

HENRY    Paris.

DOLLY    I knew Henry in Paris. We're old friends. Did you know that, John?

HENRY    Ah, Paris.

DOC    Take a pill, Henry. [HENRY *takes a pill*]

DOLLY    I loved it. I had a good job and a lot of respect. Stayed up almost every night to watch the sun go down over a glass of wine. I loved it. But I had to leave because of the Fascists.

DOC    I heard you had to leave because you got the clap.

DOLLY    Henry, you pig's ass. What have you been telling him?

HENRY    Paris. Sunset.

DOLLY    Answer me, Henry.

HENRY    Sunrise. Peace. Prime of life. Gena with the big boobs. Wine. Sex. Good friends. Cunts. Women. Tits.

DOLLY    Henry!

DOC    Leave him alone. He's trying to make a come-back.

DOLLY    Whatever he told you — it's a lie. I've always lived by my wits and I've never had to hustle. It's a lie.

DOC    [DOC *points gun to her head*] Clap. [*Pause.* DOLLY *flips nervously through her album*]

DOLLY    Here he is, John. The darling who makes the world go round. Little Ivanhoe.

DOC    Who?

DOLLY    Our son, John. Your son. Blushing, bouncing Ivanhoe Jones. Our son.

STEIN    [*standing*] I had no son.

DOLLY    Damn these interruptions.

STEIN    I had no daughter. My children were all expatriates. Geniuses. They looked up at me from their mattresses on the floor and saw the Great Mother of all art. Cubism. Paris.
     [*She sits*]

HENRY    Paris.

DOLLY    Look at him, John. Here he is swimming across Lake Erie. He was only twelve. And in this one, look. He's only sixteen. Climbing Mount Fuji. And this one, taken a bit later. Surrounded by all those awe-struck Orientals. They loved him, John.

DOC    Why's his last name Jones?

DOLLY    He changed it. Look here he is invading Korea. A lot of people think he won that war for us all by himself. And here he is surrounded by more Orientals. These ones are dead. Oh, John ...

DOC    Why'd he change it?

DOLLY   He needed a name with a ring to it.

DOC   Why?

DOLLY   Because of his profession. Oh John, he's a truly remarkable person. All blood and action. Always reversing the odds and emerging victorious. A lovely strapper. Of course, I haven't seen him for awhile. He had worlds to conquer and I didn't want to get in his way. But I'm sure he's still a gigantic darling. And he came from us. You and me. A baby. My child. Rushing out of my womb like a streak of gold. The only real thing I've ever had. Thank God. Lovely God. Sympathetic God.

> [**MASONETTES** *come on. Heavy on the lipstick. Sing* Dolly's Hymn.* *Everyone is looking slightly upward. During hymn —* **ALADDIN** *comes on and sits quietly in a corner ... and* **SARA** *enters, pregnant.* **MASONETTES** *finish. Go behind the bar and chew gum*]

SARA   Only two months and already kicking like it was going to be born tomorrow.

DOLLY   Your baby will be a weakling half-breed. You should have it aborted. I'll do it for you if you want.

> [*Abortion is a bad word in this play for some reason. Everyone groans, mutters or shouts their disapproval.* **MITCH** *enters. Blows a whistle. Silence*]

MITCH   Ladies and gentlemen. It is with nothing but honour that I present to you, my boss. The greatest golfer in the history of the game. Winner of the American Open, The Masters, The P.G.A., The Tennessee Invitational, The Rudy Vallee Tournament of Stars, and the Armed Forces Veterans Handicap Cup. The only golfer to ever single hole twice on the front nine. And the holder of the record for most eagles on a par five with an elbowed fairway. A goodwill emissary for his government on numerous occasions and a champion of the people. In short, a hero. A real hero.

> [*They all rise. Applaud semi-consciously. Realize what they're doing and sit*]

My boss. Mr. Ivanhoe Jones.

DOLLY   My son. My boy.

*Music — Steven Jack, Lyrics — George Walker

[**IVANHOE JONES** *enters. He is immediately hideous. A short, sprawling mass with a deformed face. (a victim of fire?) A partial hunchback with an oversized head. What little hair he has is white. He is very, very old.* **SARA** *screams. Faints. Bedlam and general fear all around. With the exception of* **DOLLY** *who runs to embrace him*] Oh baby, you're a sight for sore eyes.

STEIN    Mother!

HENRY    Get back. It's the demon whale! My lampoon, Mr. Starbuck. [*Raises his arm*]

DOC    [*drawing his gun*] Get out of the way, Dolly. I'm gonna put him out of his misery.

DOLLY    No.

STEIN    Mother! It's my mother! [*She hides her head*]

DOLLY    What's wrong with you people. This is my son.

DOC    Get out of the way!

DOLLY    No. [*To* **IVANHOE**] Don't worry, honey. They're out of their minds.

IVANHOE    Snork*

DOLLY    What was that?

IVANHOE    Snork. Trebble. Uh.

DOLLY    I know. I know, sugar. He wants me to remind you that he is an American citizen.

IVANHOE    Enff. Snork.

DOLLY    And a veteran. Now all of you sit down and try to be polite. John, put your gun on the table. This is your son.

DOC    Good God, woman. What are you saying. Are you trying to embarrass me.

DOLLY    He's your son!

IVANHOE    Snork. [*Scratches his crotch*]

DOC    All right. Everyone out of the way. This wise ass freak is gonna get a bullet right in the mouth. If I can find his mouth. Christ, will you look at that face.

HENRY    I see his mouth, Doc. It's under his ear.

DOLLY    That's a war wound, Henry. Now sit down and shut up.

*IVANHOE has a language. The language consists of 'Snork,' 'Trebble,' 'Rufe,' 'Enff,' and 'Uh.' Nothing more. Nothing less.

DOC        I want to kill him. I'm gonna kill him.

DOLLY      You. Sit down and shut up too!

           [**DOLLY** *marches to* **DOC**. *Takes the gun from his hand and puts*
           *it on his table.* **DOC** *is stunned, looks around, then sits*]
           There. Now make yourself at home, son. These people are all
           friends. They all love and admire you like I do.

           [**IVANHOE** *shakes his head. Whispers to* **MITCH**]

MITCH      My boss thanks you from the bottom of his heart.

           [**IVANHOE** *belches. Salivates.* **HENRY** *howls. Laughs*
           *grotesquely. Pounds his chest.* **STEIN** *slaps* **HENRY** *across the*
           *face*]

DOLLY      Go ahead, love. [**IVANHOE** *whispers to* **MITCH**]

MITCH      And he says he wants you all to know the truth. [*To* **IVANHOE**]
           What truth? [*Whispers*] Really? [*Whispers*] Are you sure?
           [*Whispers*] All right.

DOLLY      Don't you worry, Ivanhoe. Just speak right out.

MITCH      Well, you see, it's a matter of profession. Mr. Jones, well he's,
           like I told ya — a golfer — the best — well, ah, he was. But, well
           the tide changes. Right? And the boss — well people forget ...
           [*Whispers*] Something went wrong. He doesn't want I should
           bother you with details. But it's like this, kinda. He has to change
           professions.

DOLLY      Oh no. Poor darling.

MITCH      And he needs time to get — what is it ... [*Whispers*] Expertise — in
           his new profession. Ya see the boss — Mr. Jones — he got kinda
           used to the limelight and when ... [*Whispers*] He says the best
           way is to show you.

DOLLY      [*to* **IVANHOE**] Oh yes, baby dear. You go ahead and show us
           anything you want.

MITCH      Wait. [*From his golf bag* **MITCH** *takes a trench coat, and a*
           *microphone.* **IVANHOE** *puts on the coat, whispers to* **MITCH**]
           Yeah ... yeah ... Okay.

           [*Taking* **IVANHOE** *downstage, he returns with tape-recorder.*
           *Sits*]
           We could use better lights. Lights are important, ya see.

           [*A green spot on* **IVANHOE**. *The rest of the stage is in darkness*]
           Yeah. Well, we've got a lot of kinks to iron out. So don't expect
           too much. [*To* **IVANHOE**] Ready?

IVANHOE    Rufe.

MITCH    Oh. Wait.

> [**MITCH** *runs into the spot. Puts a hat (Fedora) on* **IVANHOE**'s
> *head. Taps him on the shoulder. Retreats*]

A one, a two, a three …

> [*Recording of* The Good Life *by some male singer with full
> orchestral support.* **IVANHOE** *mimes the song as if he were in a
> nightclub act. Appropriate gestures to the audience and the
> orchestra.* **MASONETTES** *are swaying in the background. On
> for a decent interval, at least two minutes. They all stand and
> join in for the last part of the song. A shot.* **IVANHOE** *drops to
> his knees. Head bowed. Recording stops.*
>         [*Blackout.. Pause. Lights*]
> *All those who were there before are standing in a line.
> Wide-eyed, with one hand over his or her mouth. Pause. Enter*
> **AHRUN** *and the* **SERVANT**. **AHRUN** *is extremely drunk. The*
> **SERVANT** *extremely sober*]

SERVANT    Look at them. Is it a game?

AHRUN    Probably. What's that? [*The line-up dissolves. People relax*]

SERVANT    It's the demon!

AHRUN    It's no demon, you old fool. It's a man. See why he is on his
knees.

SERVANT    He's been shot.

AHRUN    Is he dead?

SERVANT    He's dying.

AHRUN    [*giddily*] So it's not enough to be inhuman, arrogant and
completely opposed to the natural order of things. Now they've
become murderers.

SERVANT    Logical.

AHRUN    I didn't ask you.

SERVANT    Logical, nevertheless. Look for yourself.

> [**AHRUN** *goes to* **IVANHOE**. *He becomes suddenly sober. The*
> **SERVANT** *suddenly drunk*]

AHRUN    [*groans*] Poor wretch! [*To* **SERVANT**] See what's wrong with my
daughter.

SERVANT    Okay.

AHRUN    Terrible sad man. Can you hear me?

> [**IVANHOE** *gurgles.* **AHRUN** *bends to listen*]

A sad story.

SERVANT    Your daughter has passed out.

| | |
|---|---|
| AHRUN | Take her to the tent. She's going to give birth to a monster. [SERVANT laughs] What's so funny? |
| SERVANT | I don't know. |
| AHRUN | Get out of here. |
| SERVANT | Okay. [SERVANT *takes* SARA *out with difficulty.* AHRUN *slowly goes to the others. He walks up and down in front of them. Looks into their eyes. Stops. Stares off*] |
| AHRUN | Murderers. [*Pause*] My daughter. My grandchild. A monster. Ugly. Deformed. Useless. Embarrassing. |
| | [*The gun is on the table.* DOLLY *hands it to* DOC. DOC *hands it to* AHRUN. AHRUN *hesitates. Takes it. Puts it to his head. Suddenly drops it*] |
| | No. Just who do you think you are? [*They all laugh*] |
| DOC | [*to others*] Me first. [*To* AHRUN] I am what I have made myself. |
| AHRUN | And what's that? |
| DOC | The death wish turned outward. Suicide gone mad. |
| AHRUN | No. I don't want to hear that stuff. |
| DOC | Okay. I'm a man who doesn't take shit. |
| AHRUN | A killer. [*Pause*] |
| DOC | I killed my son. |
| AHRUN | Why? |
| DOC | He looked like me when I get up in the morning. He looked like me when I'm old, ugly and very short. He deserved to get killed. Honest. |
| AHRUN | Murderer. |
| STEIN | I am. And I was and will be even after I am not what I am now. And I am. |
| AHRUN | What? |
| STEIN | A nice Jewish girl from Pennsylvania. Daughter of a fine old man. Poetess, Cubist. The greatest prose writer ever to be emulated. [*To* AHRUN] I was unable to give an answer because no one could tell me what the question was. I killed her. |
| AHRUN | Doc killed him. |
| STEIN | I killed her. |
| AHRUN | Why? |
| STEIN | Because I didn't like its structure. Its form was not clear and its texture was cloudy. It was imperfect. And it had a nasty bulge in its pants. |
| AHRUN | You're crazy. |

STEIN     I am of course. I am.

HENRY     I am. Me too. I am.

AHRUN     Be quiet. I've heard enough.

HENRY     I'm the early bird who can't find the fucking worm.

AHRUN     Enough.

HENRY     The first unsponsored explorer into the poetics of orgasm. The exploited little drip of women's whims — I am the ex-husband-ex-student, ex-American, ex-man, ex-writer. Exed right out of existence. Then exed and exed again. The unloved, non-loved, no love, low love, ho ho and lonely love unloved man. I would kill anyone for absolutely no reason at all. And who could blame me. I did it. Punish me.

AHRUN     No.

HENRY     I'm the one.

DOLLY     I am.

AHRUN     Enough.

DOLLY     A pretty girl. A lovely gracious lady. I couldn't kill, not me. But if I did there would be a good reason.

AHRUN     But you're his mother.

DOLLY     [*calmly*] The mother who wanted a beautiful baby. The mother who gave birth to mutation. A hunchback. A dwarf. I killed him. My baby.

     [AHRUN *lowers his head.* ALADDIN *who has been standing motionless walks to him*]

ALADDIN     Forgive me. For I became totally confused.

AHRUN     What?

ALADDIN     I murdered the beast.

AHRUN     Chaos. [AHRUN *lowers his head again*]

DOLLY     I did.

MITCH     I did. [*Smiles*] I did.

ALL     I did!

     [*Pause. They all move slowly to their tables. Sit. Lights down. Spot on* IVANHOE. *He struggles to his feet. Clutching his microphone. Tries to snap his fingers to create a beat. In pain. Still trying to regain his form. Stomps his foot.* 'Oh, the good life!' *Music winds down*]

IVANHOE     Snork. [*He sinks to his knees*]

AHRUN     Chaos.

           [*Blackout*]

# Part 2, Scene 17

*Banquet. Minuet. Much liquor all around.* DOC *and* SARA *are embracing.* DOC *is nibbling on her ear. In one hand he has a bottle of whiskey.* HENRY *sits knitting a large shawl.* DOLLY *watches* DOC *and* SARA. MITCH *is holding a large roast turkey on a tray.*

*At a table in the corner, the* MASONETTES. *One dressed exactly like* DOC, *one like* HENRY *and one like* STEIN.
*At another table.* AHRUN, ALADDIN, *the* SERVANT. *Motionless. Dusty. Staring off.*

MITCH *rings dinner bell. Music stops.* [*All conversation is jolly and elegantly delivered. Everyone is white-haired, grey-haired or yellow-skinned. All have either aged or rotted. Despite dialogue which might indicate otherwise, no one moves until* STEIN *enters.*

| | |
|---|---|
| MITCH | Henry. |
| HENRY | Huh? |
| MITCH | What part of the bird would you like? |
| HENRY | Nothing. |
| DOLLY | Come on, Henry, you have to eat. |
| HENRY | I'm five sighs away from the grave. And you want to breast feed me. |
| DOLLY | I already have a son. A wonderful son. |
| HENRY | Don't give me that. Your kind of silly maternal instincts are never satisfied. You want to expand the family. And I'm not having any part of it. You hear? |
| DOLLY | Oh, just hush up and eat. |
| SARA | Yes, please eat, Henry. |
| HENRY | All right, all right! I'll have some stuffing. |
| DOC | If you're gonna take the trouble of eating then you might as well eat meat. |
| HENRY | I can't eat meat, you stupid asshole. My teeth are falling out. |
| DOC | I never hit a cripple, Henry. It's part of my credo. And it's the only thing that's saving you. |
| HENRY | I'm going to lie down. |

[STEIN *enters. Holding* IVANHOE *by the hand.* IVANHOE *is bleeding from the head*]

STEIN   Nobody goes anywhere. Nobody speaks. Nobody breathes. I've just had a revelation.

ALL   Hi!

STEIN   Silence. I've just come from the desert. No, I wasn't waiting for God or the Son of God, or the nephew or the second cousin of God. I was waiting for the universe to straighten up its act. I was waiting for the irrational to become rational and the contra and pro quid, pro factem of all that to become finally and crystally clear.

HENRY   Did it?

> [**DOLLY** *goes to* **IVANHOE**, *straightens his clothing. Smoothes his hair*]

STEIN   I was visited by a family of gophers. We conversed. They invited relatives. And shortly, I was surrounded by an entire herd of gophers. Further conversation. Tea was taken and we discussed aesthetics for awhile. A bit of preaching on my part, a bit on theirs. Much dialogue and interaction between me and the gophers. Good news! The world is not arbitrary. Everything is motivated. They have a doctrine. Those gophers are Moslems!

SARA   [*tipsily*] Hurray!

DOLLY   She's drunk.

SARA   I'm defenceless. [**DOC** *grabs her*]

DOLLY   I'm disgusted.

HENRY   I'm bored.

STEIN   I'm visionary. Things are occurring in pairs. Flash. Two insights. Flash. Two truths. Flash. Zing. Two holy words. Two eyes. Two brains. Two trees. Two cows ... and two roast turkeys without their legs.

SARA   I'm afraid she has the fever of the brain.

STEIN   The only route to invulnerability is in the repression of all needs and the denouncement of all desires. [*Staggers*] I'm going back into the desert to die and be reborn. If I return you'll know I've failed.

> [*She takes* **IVANHOE**. *Leaves. They all applaud*]

MITCH   She's returned three times in the last hour. You have to admit she's got class.

HENRY   [*to* **MITCH**] I'll take that stuffing now. [**MITCH** *grabs a glass*]

DOLLY   Eventually I want my son to become a rock star. I think he has what it takes.

MITCH    Bottoms up! [**DOLLY, DOC, SARA, HENRY** *all grab glasses*]

ALL    To style!!

> [*Lights fade. Pause. Lights brighten and the play reverses itself*]

ALL    To style!!

MITCH    Bottoms up.

DOLLY    Eventually I want my son to become a rock star. I think he has what it takes.

HENRY    I'll take that stuffing now.

MITCH    She's returned three times in the last hour. You have to admit she's got class.

> [*They all applaud.* **STEIN** *backs in with* **IVANHOE**. *Leaves him. Turns outward*]

STEIN    If I return you'll know I've failed.

> [*Blackout. Lights up. Everyone is staring out hard. One by one they leave. Slowly. Turning back occasionally. Staring. Music. 'Is that all there is?' Everyone is leaving slowly*]

### THE END

FACTORY THEATRE LAB

PRESENTS....

# BEYOND MOZAMBIQUE

207 Adelaide St. East
(at Jarvis)

Reservations: 921~5989

Opens May 11th, 1974
Tues.– Sun. at 8:30
& Sun. at 2:30

by
GEORGE F. WALKER

directed by
ERIC STEINER

Annalee Orr '74

*Beyond Mozambique* was first produced at Factory Theatre Lab on May 11, 1974 with the following cast:

ROCCO    Donald Davis
TOMAS    Marc Connors
OLGA    Frances Hyland
RITA    Wendy Thatcher
CORPORAL    Dean Hawes
LIDUC    David Bolt

Set designed by: Doug Robinson
Costumes by: Marti Wright
Lighting designed by: John Stammers
Directed by: Eric Steiner

*Persons*
ROCCO
TOMAS
OLGA
RITA
CORPORAL
LIDUC

*Beyond Mozambique* was revived at Factory Theatre Lab on January 3, 1978 with the following cast:

ROCCO    David Bolt
TOMAS    Peter Blais
OLGA    Barbara Gordon
RITA    Susan Purdy
CORPORAL    Miles Potter
LIDUC    Jim Henshaw

Designed by: Brian Arnott and Syvalya Elchen
Directed by: George F. Walker

# Scene 1

*Late evening. The porch and surrounding area of an old poorly
maintained colonial house. Surrounded by jungle. Cluttered
with discarded things. Old tires; machine parts; magazines and
newspapers strewn all around. To one side of the steps, a large
picnic table. To the other side,* **DOCTOR ROCCO**'s *operating
table. It has an umbrella attached to one end. Leaning against the
roof of the house, a battered telephone pole, wires hanging to the
ground.*

*A whistle from the jungle.* **ROCCO** *rushes out of the house in a lab
coat, carrying his medical bag. He looks around. Another whistle.*
**ROCCO** *goes off into the jungle toward it. Whisperings.
Commotion. Branches breaking. Muttering. Muffled drums.*
**TOMAS** *comes out of the jungle. His head is bandaged; a trace of
blood. Over his shoulder he is carrying a corpse covered by
sackcloth.* **ROCCO** *follows him.*

TOMAS   Thélo ná nikyáso éna aftokínito.

ROCCO   Who cares. Just keep going. Wait. I hear something. I said.
Wait.

TOMAS   O Kafés?

ROCCO   Shut up. Were you followed? No. You're too shrewd. Wait. No.
Nothing. Get going. [*Pushes* **TOMAS**] Get going.
    [*They start off.* **ROCCO** *looks under the corpse's sackcloth*]
Stop. [*Grabs* **TOMAS**] This corpse. It's Old Joseph. I saw him
yesterday. In good health. Put him down.
    [**TOMAS** *puts the corpse on the picnic table*]
I told you. Only dead ones. Out of graves. Graves, stupid. You
murdered him, didn't you?
    [**TOMAS** *produces a switchblade. Runs it across his own
    throat. Smiles*]
No. The knife was only for cutting open the corpses' sacks. To
check for decomposition. You've murdered Old Joseph. Look at
him lying there. I taught that old man how to play dominoes. Oh
God, he's missing a foot. Where's his foot? [**TOMAS** *shrugs.*
**ROCCO** *points to his own*] Foot. Where's Old Joseph's foot?

[**TOMAS** *nods. Undoes his coat. The foot is strung around his neck*]

TOMAS   Good luck.

ROCCO   What's wrong with you? [*Yanks it off*] Have you no respect for human life?

[*Throws the foot into the bushes*]

I'm very sad.

TOMAS   Foot.

ROCCO   How many more of them have you murdered? Never mind. I don't want to know. What's done is done. At least it's for a worthy cause. He was a man of some wisdom. He might have understood. What's done is done. Off to the lab. Pick him up.

TOMAS   [*stomps his foot petulantly*] Foot!

ROCCO   Forget it! It's sickening, I'm sad. No. I must maintain my obsession. One day they will place a huge tablet in the foyer of the city hall in Naples. 'To Doctor Enrico Rocco, a native son. A man who had the courage lacking in all other scientists of his age. It was not that he thought that human life was cheap but that he believed that the advancement of medical science was divine.'

[**TOMAS** *puts his hand on* **ROCCO**'s *shoulder*]

Oh yes. And a smaller plaque hidden in a corner. 'In memory of his clueless assistant. Tomas. Who was a scummy bastard of the first order.'

TOMAS   [*smiles*] Tomas.

[**OLGA** *comes out of the house, carrying linen and a basket full of silverware, plates, etc*]

OLGA   Oh, Enrico. I have to set that table for breakfast. Please remove the patient.

ROCCO   We were just leaving. [*To* **TOMAS**] Pick him up.

[**TOMAS** *throws the corpse over his shoulder. They start off*]

OLGA   Don't be out late, dear. The monsoons are coming.

[**ROCCO** *and* **TOMAS** *disappear around the back of the house*]

Ah. The monsoon season. A trying time. A trying time indeed.

[**OLGA** *begins to set the table, humming the Polovtsian Dances. The sound of an approaching car is heard, screeching to a halt. The porch is flooded in light. Sound of* *door opening. Door closing.* OLGA *is oblivious, going about her business.* RITA *comes on, carrying a shopping bag. Her hands and arms are covered with blood. The rest of the scene is dealt with in the most casual of manners*]

RITA  Where's the Doctor.

OLGA  Out.

RITA  Goddamnit.
[*Sits on the steps. Fingers her hair back*]

OLGA  Not so much activity please. You'll stir up the mosquitoes.

RITA  Goddamnit. Have you seen the Corporal. I can't find him anywhere.

OLGA  No. What's that you're covered with?

RITA  Blood.

OLGA  From where?

RITA  His head.

OLGA  Whose head?

RITA  The priest. Father Ricci. Someone took an axe to him. I found his head outside my tent. It's in this bag. And I don't know what I'm supposed to do with it. I mean I can't carry it around forever. It's stupid.

OLGA  This joke is in poor taste, Shirley.

RITA  The name's Rita. Not Shirley. Rita. And it's no joke. Look.
[*She drops the head from the bag*]

OLGA  Yes. That's Father Ricci all right. I recognize the disapproving look. Oh. Before I forget. You're invited to breakfast tomorrow morning. It's a formal affair. In honour of my homeland. Will you come? [*Returns to setting the table*]

RITA  I'll see. I have some business to tend to.

OLGA  Well if you can make it.

RITA  Yeah. [*Pause*] Doesn't this scare you? [*Pointing to the head*] This.

OLGA  My dreams are much worse. Much worse. When I see blood in one of my dreams it's like comic relief. Does it scare you?

RITA  Well, it doesn't seem real. I mean no more real than the movies. [*Looks at her arms*] Stage blood looks the same way. That's not what bothers me. What bothers me is why it was put outside my tent. I don't need the action. Question is. Who's the one that thinks I do.
[CORPORAL *steps out of the bushes. Old Joseph's foot is tied*

*around the blade of his machete*]

CORPORAL    The question is this. Does that head have anything to do with this foot?

OLGA    Lance. Have you been lurking around my bedroom window again? You know Enrico doesn't like it.

[**CORPORAL** *goes to the head. Kneels*]

CORPORAL    Different people. My guess is that the foot belongs to one of the sub species.

RITA    Oh, I get it. Two murders.

CORPORAL    Three murders. The guy who Father Ricci replaced. Father what-sisface.

RITA    Carson.

OLGA    Oh yes. I remember. The one who ran away.

CORPORAL    Wrong. I found his body deep in the jungle this afternoon. Nailed to a tree.

RITA    A priest killer. Oh that's really bizarre.

OLGA    Lance, you're invited to breakfast tomorrow. And will you please dress.

CORPORAL    Uh-huh. This foot. This foot doesn't fit in. And I don't like that. No. I just don't like this foot. [*Thinks*] Right. One thing at a time.
[*Throws foot into the jungle. There is mumbling from the bushes. They all react.* **CORPORAL** *draws his gun, walks into the bushes. We hear thrashing. Screaming. And finally two gun shots.* **OLGA** *and* **RITA** *are looking at each other, slightly confused, slightly disgusted. The* **CORPORAL** *casually returns, wiping blood from the blade of his machete*]
Subversives. [*Everyone nods*] That keeps them away.
[*The ladies nod. They giggle just a bit*]
Relax. You're in good hands.
[*They all look at each other. They all smile.* **OLGA** *backs into the house.* **RITA** *begins to laugh loudly.* **CORPORAL** *begins to laugh boyishly, starting towards* **RITA**]

[*Blackout*]

# Scene 2

*Morning. Waiting for the guests. The table is set lavishly.*
**ROCCO**, *pacing back and forth on the ground in front of the porch,*
*is wearing an old tuxedo.* **OLGA** *is sitting in her chair on the*
*porch, reading a letter. She is wearing a full-length black dress*
*with a collar.*

ROCCO   Like a boulder crushing my skull. Twenty-five years spent
thrashing about in the wilderness. And then I wake up one day
like a baby in its crib. Sucking my thumb and pissing my pants.
Another wasted night. Twenty-five years long. Where are we!?

OLGA   I didn't say anything.

ROCCO   Neither did I.

OLGA   Masha writes such good letters. Social enough to satisfy the
mind. Bittersweet enough to appease the memory.

ROCCO   Here. Really here. I don't believe it. And then there's the wasted
time. The interruptions.

OLGA   London agrees with her. She writes her letters in English now.
But somehow they still have a Russian accent.

ROCCO   Interruptions.

OLGA   Do you know how much I miss her.

ROCCO   Interruptions. Caring for the sick. Why for once can't the sick
care for themselves? Don't they know I'm busy. Where am I?
I'm not at the place I came to. The place I came to is somewhere
else. It's quieter there. A man gets work done there without
worrying about his conscience. My god. My poor conscience.

OLGA   Enrico.

ROCCO   [*to* OLGA] Woman. Why are you pestering me? What harm have I
done you lately. Do I complain that you hum the Polovtsian
Dances in your sleep. No, I grant you your oblivion. And all I ask
in return is that you bow completely out of the picture until my
work is finished.

OLGA   You were raving. [*Pause*]

ROCCO   Tell me I am a genius. There's no one around. Olga, tell me. That
if I had been born two centuries earlier and lived three times as
long as anyone else I would have discovered all the cures now
known to modern medicine. I don't ask much, Olga. But a mind

like mine has a great appetite. It even needs flattery. Tell me. Am I amazing?

OLGA   Of course.

ROCCO   Somehow it doesn't seem like enough. Olga, I have something to tell you. No. Forget it.

OLGA   Would you like to read my sister's letter?

ROCCO   No. I can't stomach the way she manages to swoon even on a piece of paper.

OLGA   She misses Moscow.

ROCCO   Everyone misses Moscow. I miss it occasionally myself. And I've never been there.

OLGA   The letter contains good news.

[ROCCO *gestures for her to continue*]

Your friend Livarno has won the Nobel Prize.

ROCCO   [*groans lightly. Bites his knuckles*] I know. We saw it in the newspaper last month. His picture covered the entire front page. Large vacant eyes. And a smile like a sheep. He didn't exist in Naples and even now, covering the entire front page of a newspaper, he does not really exist. His Nobel Prize for Science is a bad joke.

OLGA   You're jealous.

ROCCO   Stupidity fits you sometimes like a glove.

OLGA   [*getting up*] It's time for my nap.

ROCCO   Livarno is a mediocre mind. His accomplishments seem important only because he is surrounded by apes.

OLGA   Then maybe you should consider going back. You could always disguise yourself. And as for me –

ROCCO   And as for you what? You have all you need.

OLGA   I don't know what I need. I do know what I have.

ROCCO   What do you have?

OLGA   My marriage. My history. And my original Renoir.

ROCCO   Exactly. Everything you need. The question is answered in the best way possible. By evasion. We stay here.

OLGA   For how long?

ROCCO   The world and I will collide at the proper moment. Everything in time.

OLGA   I don't like that expression! I blinked my eyes once and half a century passed. I found myself in a square in St. Petersburg surrounded by young men and women all looking exactly alike. I was wearing a ball gown and everyone thought I was about to perform an historical drama. Immediately I gave up.

ROCCO    I've always wondered what happened to your passion.

OLGA    What was left I gave to you.

ROCCO    Thank you.

OLGA    Not at all. I scarcely miss it now.

ι    [*The* CORPORAL *comes on in full dress, R.C.M.P. uniform. Without speaking, he goes to the table. Takes his seat*]

ROCCO    What in God's name is that outfit all about?

OLGA    Lance was with the R.C.M.P. before he came to work here.

ROCCO    What's the R.C.M.P.?

OLGA    I'll explain later.

ROCCO    How'd he get here? I didn't hear his motorcycle.

OLGA    Some of the locals dismantled it. And Lance doesn't know how to put it back together.

ROCCO    The man is a clown. The only policeman in the area is a full-fledged clown. That is the most ridiculous uniform I have ever seen in my life.

OLGA    Shush. He's very insecure. [*Goes to* CORPORAL] Good morning, Lance. Nice of you to attend.

CORPORAL    Sure. [*Quietly*] Am I over-dressed? It's the only formal thing I've got.

OLGA    No. You look fine. Almost dashing.

ROCCO    [*approaching them*] Come on now. Let's get this over with.

CORPORAL    Good morning, doctor.

ROCCO    Is it? [*He sits*]

OLGA    [*sitting*] Where is Tomas?

ROCCO    Sleeping.

OLGA    Well who gave him permission to do that?

ROCCO    I did. I need him well rested.

OLGA    Unfair. The agreement was that I have him during the day and you have him during the night. Who is going to serve breakfast?

ROCCO    I don't know. Improvise.

CORPORAL    [*stands*] What do you and your boy do during the night anyway, Doctor?

ROCCO    [*stands*] We make house calls. Now take off your hat. My wife has gone to a great deal of trouble to create the proper atmosphere. [*Sits*]

CORPORAL    [*removes his hat*] Sorry. [*Sits. Pause*]

OLGA    Enrico. The breakfast.

ROCCO    Be patient.

OLGA    But —

ROCCO    Be patient.

CORPORAL    Well now —

ROCCO    That goes for you too.

       [*Long pause.* OLGA *sits restless;* CORPORAL, *embarrassed;* ROCCO, *patient*]

OLGA    Excuse me.

       [*They all stand.* OLGA *smiles. Goes into house.* ROCCO *and* CORPORAL *sit. Long pause.* ROCCO *is looking the* CORPORAL *over*]

ROCCO    How's your malaria?

CORPORAL    Comes and goes.

ROCCO    How often?

CORPORAL    More often all the time. I think I almost died last week from the fever. I was having having visions of wheat.

ROCCO    Are you getting your transfer?

CORPORAL    My superiors say I have to prove myself here first. And with all these murders going on and that bunch of subversives running around blowing things up, well, it doesn't make me look very good. Why are you smiling?

ROCCO    I give you two months. Unless you can escape this climate. Two months at the most.

CORPORAL    You're joking.

ROCCO    I joke with friends. To people like you I dish out the ruthless truth. You're a dead man.

CORPORAL    Then cure me.

ROCCO    No.

CORPORAL    It's because I did your wife, isn't it? Don't hold it against me forever, for Christ's sake. I mean, goddamnit man. She came to me.

       [ROCCO *produces a switchblade with incredible speed and*

*efficiency. Puts the blade under the* **CORPORAL'**s *chin*]

ROCCO   I am not an impotent man, you son-of-a-bitch. There are plenty of men who can't do their wives who aren't impotent. They just can't do their wives. For reasons none of your business. For reasons no one knows.

CORPORAL   Put the knife away, Doctor. I've got something to tell you.

ROCCO   Be careful, Corporal.

CORPORAL   I talked to Father Ricci the night before he was killed. He'd been doing a little investigating of his own. Seems he found out about this Italian doctor who was so good at his job that he became top dog in one of those fancy Nazi hospitals. They're still looking for him.

ROCCO   You repeat that once. To anyone. And I'll slice you up.

CORPORAL   Listen, Rocco. You can get away with robbing graves here. It's a petty crime. Just like the little bribes you all know I take. But anything more will upset the balance. Don't do anything to upset the balance. Understand?

[*They stare at each other*]

ROCCO   [*chuckles, puts the knife away*] Ah mother of Jesus. I am only a simple country doctor. Leave me to my business in peace and you'll be fine.

[**OLGA** *comes out with four glasses of orange juice on a tray*]

OLGA   I see that Shirley still hasn't arrived. A typical display of rudeness.

ROCCO   Rita will be late. She had a business meeting.

[**OLGA** *is serving the juice*]

CORPORAL   What kind of business?

ROCCO   Ask *her.*

OLGA   Is it true that she's making pornographic movies with the natives?

CORPORAL   That's news to me.

OLGA   Well perhaps it's just a malicious rumour. I hear so many.

ROCCO   From whom?

OLGA   Many different sources, Enrico. [*Raises her glass*] To dear Russia.

[**ROCCO** *stands.* **CORPORAL** *knocks his glass over*]

What's wrong Lance?

CORPORAL  Sorry.

ROCCO  The Corporal is having trouble coping with imaginary problems.

    [**ROCCO** *and* **CORPORAL** *are staring hard at each other*]

CORPORAL  Two murders. Possibly three. People mucking about with government property. Strange comings. Strange goings. Mysterious sounds in the night. Add all that up and tell me what it sounds like to you.

OLGA  'Les Miserables' by Victor Hugo. [*They look at her*] Excuse me.
    [*She stands.* **CORPORAL** *and* **ROCCO** *stand.* **OLGA** *smiles,*
    *goes into the house*]

CORPORAL  Victor Hugo my bassoon. It sounds like anarchy. It sounds like insurrection.

ROCCO  Why are you telling me all this?

CORPORAL  You were seen at three o'clock this morning sitting cross-legged in the jungle behind your house. Wearing an old army helmet and cradling a carbine in your lap.

ROCCO  What were you doing sneaking around my house at that hour?

CORPORAL  Subversives do their best work before dawn.

ROCCO  Ah. Are you a subversive?

CORPORAL  Just answer the question. What were you doing out there?

ROCCO  Maybe I was out there asleep. But I haven't slept for years. Maybe I was awake and can't remember. But that is unlikely. Or maybe I was mistaken for another. Which is probably too far-fetched. All right. I was really out there like you say. Wide awake. Suspiciously dressed. And armed to the teeth.

CORPORAL  Why?

ROCCO  [*standing*] None of your business.

CORPORAL  [*standing*] Now get this you mother-fucker. My life is on the line and no stupid wop quack is gonna ball it up for me.

ROCCO  Va fungu! [*Producing his switchblade*]

CORPORAL  The same to you! [*Drawing his gun*]
    [**OLGA** *comes out, carrying cups and a coffee pot on a tray*]

OLGA  Coffee?

CORPORAL  Sure.

ROCCO  Why not.
    [**OLGA** *pours the coffee. The weapons are put away*]

OLGA  Things aren't going well, are they? But then again they never do.

If only Tomas was operating with all his faculties. I tried to wake him but he wouldn't budge. Enrico, where did he get that teddy bear he's sleeping with?

ROCCO   Rita gave it to him.

OLGA   Are they having an affair?

ROCCO   Anything's possible.

OLGA   Rumour has it that they are. But how many rumours can one believe. Very few. Very few indeed.

CORPORAL   [*opening his collar*] I don't feel so good. [*He staggers a bit*]

OLGA   [*raises her cup*] Forever remembered. Forever lost. Those brittle Russian nights.

  [*They drink.* CORPORAL *spits his out*]

  Well if you'd said so earlier, Lance, I would have served you tea.

CORPORAL   [*tears open his tunic*] Fever!

  [*The* CORPORAL *falls on the ground, groaning, pulling at his hair*]

OLGA   Goodness. It does come on suddenly, doesn't it? [*To* ROCCO] Help him.

ROCCO   What's that?

OLGA   Help him. It's his malaria.

ROCCO   So it is. So it is.

  [*Pours himself another cup of coffee*]

OLGA   [*starting towards the house*] I'll go get him a cold towel.

ROCCO   Get me my flask while you're in there, will you?

  [LIDUC *comes out of the jungle, carrying a valise, covered with mud up to his chest. He is casually dressed in a windbreaker and slacks*]

LIDUC   Excuse me. Can you direct me to the mission? [*Smiles*]

  [*They all turn toward him*]

CORPORAL   [*pointing hysterically*] Assassin! Oh Jesus an assassin!

  [*He rushes* LIDUC *screaming 'Assassin, assassin.' Throws him up against* ROCCO's *operating table. Turns him around. Frisks him*]

LIDUC   Please.

CORPORAL   Don't move.

LIDUC   [*to* ROCCO] Is this a mistake?

ROCCO   Corporal, what are you doing?

CORPORAL    [*to* **LIDUC**] All right. Strip.

LIDUC    I beg your pardon.

CORPORAL    Off with your clothes. I wanna see you naked.
[**LIDUC** *undoes his jacket. And we see his collar and his crucifix*]

OLGA    Oh, Lance. He's a priest.

CORPORAL    He ain't white. He's one of them. A mulatto or something.

LIDUC    No. Chinese. Half Chinese.

CORPORAL    Shut up.

LIDUC    I'll show you some identification. [*Produces a small card*] My name is LiDuc. Father LiDuc. [*Hands* **CORPORAL** *the card*]

CORPORAL    You're a goddamn chink! Goddamn — [*Falls all over* **LIDUC**] Fever.

LIDUC    Oh my God. I mean. Oh. That is. This is. Oh. [*Frees himself from the* **CORPORAL**'s *grasp*]

OLGA    Here father. Some coffee.

LIDUC    Yes. Thank you. [*Takes it. Trembling*]

OLGA    Please excuse the Corporal. He suffers from several viruses.
[**LIDUC** *nods. Hands coffee to the* **CORPORAL**]
Oh. How nice. Won't you sit down?

LIDUC    Yes. Thank you. [*He sits somewhere*] Thank you.

OLGA    [*to* **ROCCO**] Breakfast is a disaster. I should have expected it. Actually I did expect it. But I was hoping to be surprised.

ROCCO    [*to* **LIDUC**] Difficult journey? [*No response*] The mud! On your clothes!

LIDUC    Yes. I stepped into a quagmire. I'm a bit myopic, you see. And I lost my glasses in a brief encounter with a wild pig.

ROCCO    People don't usually get out of quicksand once they're in.

LIDUC    No. Well I wouldn't have either, I suspect. I spent two entire days clinging to a vine. And then this native gentleman came along and pulled me out.

OLGA    You must be very hungry.

LIDUC    No, the native gentleman took me to his home and fed me.

ROCCO    Did you talk to him?
[**LIDUC** *stands. Turns toward the* **CORPORAL**]

LIDUC    I would like an apology from you. I think it is only fair.
[**CORPORAL** *waves stupidly*]

ROCCO    I said, did you talk to him?

[**LIDUC** *turns slowly back toward* **ROCCO**]

**LIDUC**   Yes. Not much though. He was a bit reticent.

**ROCCO**   What did he tell you?

**LIDUC**   I don't understand.

**ROCCO**   What do you know.

**LIDUC**   Oh. I know that Father Ricci is dead. I was to have been his assistant, you see. And I know that he is a policeman. And that you are a doctor. He made no mention of the lady, though.

**OLGA**   I keep a low profile.

**ROCCO**   My wife, Olga.

**OLGA**   My husband, Enrico Rocco, M.D.

**LIDUC**   Good. Introductions. [*Shaking everyone's hand*] I am Father LiDuc. Until they send Father Ricci's replacement I will be in charge of the mission.

[**OLGA** *grabs* **ROCCO**'s *sleeve. Directs his attention outward*]

**ROCCO**   [*smiles*] Oh, I'm afraid not.

**LIDUC**   What's that?

**ROCCO**   [*points*] Look.

[*They are all staring off towards us*]

**LIDUC**   A fire.

[*The* **CORPORAL** *has recovered sufficiently to express delight*]

**CORPORAL**   [*chuckling*] Ah. Too bad.

**OLGA**   [*to* **LIDUC**] Your mission.

**CORPORAL**   Well, I guess I better get over there. [*Chuckles again*]

**LIDUC**   I'll come too. Doctor?

**ROCCO**   What?

**LIDUC**   Are you coming? Someone might be injured.

**ROCCO**   Impossible. No one ever goes near the place anymore.

[**LIDUC** *starts out towards us*]

**CORPORAL**   Not that way. Too dangerous. Follow me.

[*The* **CORPORAL** *is deciding which is the longest, most pleasant route. Finally he slaps* **LIDUC** *jovially on the back. Gestures for him to follow and starts off*]

**LIDUC**   [*Backing off*] It was nice meeting you.

**OLGA**   Yes. Come again soon. And you can look at my original Renoir. It's superb. Like a dove in orgasm.

[**OLGA** *waves. The* **CORPORAL** *and* **LIDUC** *are gone*]

He seems so innocent.

ROCCO    Eh. Sure.

OLGA    Enrico. Who set that fire?

ROCCO    I don't know. Honestly.

OLGA    Thank goodness for that at least.

ROCCO    [*chuckles*] You're still standing guard over my soul, woman.

OLGA    Habit. I'm going in for a nap.

ROCCO    Send Tomas out to me.

OLGA    If I can wake him up.

ROCCO    The secret is to apply pressure to his head. At the point where the blood stain is the brightest.

> [OLGA *Nods. Goes inside.* ROCCO *produces notebook and pen. Writes something*]

Who'd expect to find so many social obligations in the midst of such desolation.

> [*A scream from the house*]

Tomas!

> [*Muttering from the house*]

Tomas! Get out here!

> [TOMAS *rushes out of the house, wearing an oversized lab coat, rubbing his bandaged head. There is more blood showing.* ROCCO *hands him a piece of paper and his knife*]

I need what is written on that paper by tonight.

TOMAS    O'Ponokéfalos.

ROCCO    That's Greek. You're regressing.

TOMAS    Yais. My haid.

ROCCO    What?

TOMAS    O'Ponokéfalos.

ROCCO    Headache?

TOMAS    Yais. My brain. Kséhasis. Forget. I forget.

ROCCO    Of course you do. But stop worrying. You're lucky to be alive. You had a severe wound in your brain. You understand?

TOMAS    Sometimes.

ROCCO    Almost totally destroyed. I have fixed. Maybe all. Maybe just some. A great miracle nevertheless. Don't worry. Here. Aspirin.

TOMAS    [*suspiciously*] Efharisto.

ROCCO    Now go about my business. You are not my only concern. Be careful. Get going!

> [ROCCO *points to paper and knife. Gives* TOMAS *a push.*

**TOMAS** *takes three or four quick paces, almost running.*
*Grasps his head. Groans. Falls into a dead faint*]
Basta! Basta! No! You don't understand. No one understands.
Existence is thrust. You get sick. You get cured. There is no room
for relapse. Never mind. [*Grabbing the paper from* **TOMAS'**
*hand*] I'll do it myself.

    [*Takes off his coat. Produces a nylon stocking from his pants'*
    *pocket. Puts it over his head. Picks up his knife. Rushes off.*
    **TOMAS** *sits up. Looks around. Drops the aspirin on the*
    *ground. Muffled drums*]

           [*Blackout*]

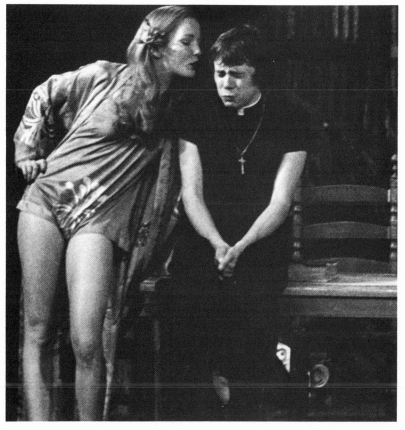

## Scene 3

*Evening.* **RITA** *and* **TOMAS** *sitting on the steps. Both have their chins in their palms. A long silence.* **RITA** *blows down into her blouse.*

**RITA**   I'll never get used to this heat. It just whacks me out.
            [**TOMAS** *produces a small fold-out fan from inside his shirt. Fans* **RITA** *slowly*]
            Ah, thanks. Hey. What's wrong with you anyway? Are you in a funk?

**TOMAS**   Funk. Sad.

**RITA**   I know. I know. It's not easy. Ah, you're bleeding again.
            [*She touches his wound. He groans*]
            I'm sorry.

**TOMAS**   Funk.

**RITA**   Yeah. Me too. I miss my man. Did I ever tell you about him? A winner. A six foot smile. The only genuine winner I've ever known in my life.

**TOMAS**   Rub.

**RITA**   Sure thing. [*Massages the back of his neck*] He's the guy who is going to make my movie. Not porn. I did porn in New York. This one is going to be a classic. It'll have sex. But it'll be sex with class. No pubics. That's what I'm doing here, you know. Research. I'm immersing myself in the place. Digging in. You know. So that when we make the movie I'll come across super real. I play a stupid slut who has always wanted to be an actress. It's a great script. It needs rewrites but basically it's a great script. I know I've told you all this before, but it's just that if I don't keep saying it I'll forget it's the truth.

**TOMAS**   Rub.

**RITA**   Yeah. Sure. [*Continues his massage*] Anyway, the Doctor thinks it's a joke. You know, 'cause I've been here for years, one year, and Chad, that's my man's name, still hasn't shown up. The Doctor's an asshole sometimes. He has no idea how much dough you need to make a film. I mean as soon as Chad gets outa prison he's going to get right back to work on raising the money. God I miss him. He never was much of a letter writer. [*Pause. Looks* *around]* This place has nice sunsets. You know that? Sometimes I just pour myself a stiff gin and lean against that big tree outside my tent and just let that sun sink slowly down into the ground while I shake the ice cubes around in the glass. And when I do that I get so deeply into Rita Hayworth I could just about die.

[**TOMAS** *sighs as he slowly rubs his crotch*]

You and the Doctor are the only ones who know. I play the role for the rest of them. It's a defense mechanism. My mother taught me all about it. When you're dealing with men do it like you got two balls and you'll be one up on most of them. [*Laughs*] It works too. I've never been raped or exploited. And I couldn't stand either.

[*Voices from the jungle*]

All right! All right! Cut the crap! I'm coming! [*Silence. To* **TOMAS**] See what I mean? Be right back.

[*She goes into the jungle.* **OLGA** *comes out in her nightgown*]

OLGA    I heard voices. What was it?

[**TOMAS** *just stares at her*]

I don't like the way you look at me. Some day I'm going to tell my husband. [*Hands* **TOMAS** *a letter*] Mail that for me tomorrow. Don't forget. Someone somewhere might be contemplating suicide. And that letter could save a life.

[**OLGA** *goes back in.* **TOMAS** *rips up the letter. Throws the pieces up in the air.* **RITA** *returns, adjusting her clothing*]

RITA    They're lunatics. I don't trust them. No way do I trust them. They drink too much and they're always wiped on this weird extract they get from the root of some fruit tree. But they've got money. And they pay me well.

TOMAS    Sex?

RITA    No. That's stupid gossip. Part of my false image. I smuggle for them. Just so I can help Chad get the money for our movie.

TOMAS    Poso?

RITA    You know I don't understand Greek. Listen. How'd you like to do me a favour?

TOMAS    Poso?

RITA    I want you to cross the border for me. I'd do it myself but I've been across too many times lately and my nerves are a little jangled. Whatya say?

TOMAS    Your eyes. I love them. Like sky at night above Athens. We live in Hilton. You pay. I am always horny. Get it?

RITA    Come on. We've been through this already. That gigolo stuff must be in your past or something. What's wrong, are you hallucinating?

TOMAS    Sick.

[*Drums, very quietly*]

RITA    Bloody Doctor. Mucking around with your head. Do me a favour and I'll get him to lay off you. [*Handing him an envelope*] Here's their money. Take it. Cross the border. Give it to the man waiting in the yellow Citroen. He'll take you to a warehouse and give you a large crate. Hire a truck and put the crate in the back under some sacks of flour. When you're driving back over the border wink at the guard and say, 'The lady from Illinois has legs.'

TOMAS    [*who has been repeating odd words*] Legs.

RITA    Then drive the truck to the ruins of the mission and leave it there.

[**TOMAS** *is ogling the money in his hands.* **RITA** *stands. Helps* **TOMAS** *up. Kissing him on the forehead*]

Thanks, sweet baby.

TOMAS    Sex?

RITA    No. We did it once. Because I liked your smile. More than once is infidelity. And I could never look Chad in the eye. Besides we're friends. We've got the only real friendship around here. Let's not screw it up, eh.

[**TOMAS** *smiles. Kisses her on the cheek*]

Thanks. Now shoo.

[*Gives him a little push. He leaves. She watches him go. Lights a cigarette. Takes a couple of puffs*]

[*To the jungle*] Okay boys. You can pick them up at the ruins of the mission. Anytime after midnight.

[*Voices from the jungle.* **RITA** *counts her money. The voices annoy her*]

Is it worth it?

[*Silence.* **ROCCO** *comes on, a corpse over his shoulder. Sees* **RITA**. *Drops the corpse. Walks to her. Produces a wad of bills. Hands them to her*]

ROCCO   This is for forgetting that you saw this. Put it away. It's a great deal of money.

[*She puts the money in her blouse. Snuffs out her cigarette*]
Excuse me.

[*He is dragging the corpse around the back of the house*]
I have to get to sleep. Tomorrow is clinic day and I am expecting many patients. The fever is with us again.

[**ROCCO** *starts around the back.* **RITA** *turns back toward us. Stares silently off for a moment.* **CORPORAL** *is waiting for* **ROCCO**. *He snaps his fingers.* **ROCCO** *sighs. Gives the* **CORPORAL** *some money. Disappears. The* **CORPORAL** *is counting the money.* **RITA** *is smoking and thinking. Eventually the* **CORPORAL** *comes around the front, still counting. Sees* **RITA**. *Smiles. Puts the money in his pocket nonchalantly. Starts to circle* **RITA**, *sizing her up. Stops. Stands there making a rude clicking noise with his tongue.* **RITA** *looks at him, sizing him up. Circles him. Stops. Stomps out her cigarette. They stare at each other for a while. It is a late evening contemptuous conversation*]

CORPORAL   I've got a problem.

RITA   I'm sure you do.

CORPORAL   I'm all alone.

RITA   I know.

CORPORAL   And I need a woman.

RITA   That's too bad.

CORPORAL   Lie down for me.

RITA   Not a chance.

CORPORAL   I'll pay the going rate.

RITA   There is no going rate, Mister.

CORPORAL   You're a whore.

RITA   You're an asshole.

CORPORAL   I could force you.

RITA   No you couldn't. [*Long pause*]

CORPORAL   I've just come into a lot of money.

RITA   I know. So have I.

CORPORAL   Enough to make your movie?

RITA   Not nearly.

CORPORAL    You could be charged as an accessory.

RITA    So could you.

CORPORAL    I'm immune.

RITA    So am I.

CORPORAL    How's that?

RITA    I talked to Father Ricci the night before he was killed.

CORPORAL    Me too.

RITA    What did he tell you?

CORPORAL    What did he tell *you?*

RITA    It's a secret.

CORPORAL    Then tell me the secret. I could force you.

RITA    No you couldn't!

CORPORAL    Is it why you killed him?

RITA    No, but it might be why you killed him. [*Long pause*]

CORPORAL    Maybe it's why the doctor killed him.

RITA    Maybe. [*Pause*]

CORPORAL    Hot, isn't it?

RITA    I don't know. I never really notice it.
[*Pause.* **CORPORAL** *takes out his money. Waves it at her*]

CORPORAL    Can you use this?
[**RITA** *takes out a card. Waves it at him*]

RITA    Can you use this?

CORPORAL    What is it?

RITA    A girl. Her name and where to find her.

CORPORAL    What are you? Her pimp or something.

RITA    Her agent.

CORPORAL    Same thing.

RITA    Yeah. I guess it is.

CORPORAL    Is she good?

RITA    She has one very intriguing asset.

CORPORAL    What is it?

RITA    She's only eleven years old.

CORPORAL    I'll take her. Give me that paper.

RITA    You first.
[*Slowly he hands her the wad of bills*]
[*Counting*] Try to be gentle. She's a close friend.

CORPORAL    [*grabbing the paper*] Oh, sure. [*Starts off. Stops*] I want you to forget this. [*He leaves*]

**RITA**  I'll try.

> [**RITA** *stuffs the money in her blouse. Looking out toward us*]
> [*With style*] I'll try.
>> [*Five or six strong drum beats*]

[*Blackout*]

# Scene 4

*Morning. Bird noises. The odd very unusual one.* **LIDUC** *is standing by the operating table. He appears to be blessing it.* **ROCCO** *comes on. Abruptly throws a pail of hot water on the table. Begins to scrub it down with a brush. He is just a bit drunk.* **LIDUC** *steps back a bit.*

**ROCCO**  Where did they go?

**LIDUC**  The native lady took her child to be buried.

**ROCCO**  It was hopeless. What are you doing?

**LIDUC**  Praying for your other patients.

**ROCCO**  Hopeless. The fever. That child is just one of many.

**LIDUC**  You would give them a better chance if you were sober.

**ROCCO**  If I was sober I couldn't even look at them. [*Pause*]

**LIDUC**  The mother left you that tire as payment.

**ROCCO**  [*chuckles*] That belongs to the Corporal's motorcycle. Look around. Tires. Old magazines. All this debris. The booty of my practice. Sad, eh?

**LIDUC**  Well if they ever take your licence away you can open up a junkyard. [*Smiles*]

**ROCCO**  European wit. Where did you pick it up? Never mind. Save it for my wife. She'll relish it.

> [**LIDUC** *goes to the porch. Sits on the steps, his Bible held to his chest*]

**LIDUC**  I'm sorry if my staying with you causes inconvenience.

**ROCCO**  Just don't get in the way of my work and you'll be tolerated.

**LIDUC**  Yes. What work is that?

**ROCCO**  My experiments. I'm searching for the cure to cancer.

**LIDUC**  Which one?

**ROCCO**  All of them.

**LIDUC**  It seems like an impossible goal.

**ROCCO**  That's why I chose it.

> [**LIDUC** *closes his eyes. Sways gently back and forth. There is a bottle and a glass on the floor of the porch.* **ROCCO** *picks them up. Pours himself a long drink. Leans against the porch. Drinks*]

How can I love with such hell in my heart. And worse knowing that the hell is what keeps me going. Knowing that when I was of the age when men make those kinds of decisions I decided to steep myself in corruption. Because corruption was the only powerful force around. And now because the age of passion is dead there is no energy to reverse the decision. My baseness is my strength. The farther down I go the safer I am. [*Pause. Drinks*] Ah. But how to explain that I cannot love. [*Turns to* LIDUC] There is a tower growing in the jungle. It is the power of light and the shrewd mind of darkness. It is the culmination of all history and civilization. And it is turning my mind into soup.

    [*They stare at each other. Long pause*]

LIDUC    You need a psychiatrist.

ROCCO    There's no psychiatrist alive who could cope with me. I am the absence of God.

LIDUC    I feel obliged to answer that.

ROCCO    Ah, I'm not listening to you. Where was the Church when I needed her? I'll tell you. The world was being torn apart. Mothers walked around grinning foolishly at their children's graves. Compromise was ruining good men forever. Chronology and reason were being shot to hell. And the Church was locked up inside an old stone palace hiding under a gigantic mahogany desk with His Eminence. Do you drink?

LIDUC    I have a glass of wine each Christmas eve. A tradition.

ROCCO    A family tradition?

LIDUC    No. A tradition of my order.

ROCCO    Difficult things. Family traditions. Especially for a man in your situation. What do you do to keep the Chinese half of you loyal to tradition?

LIDUC    Nothing.

ROCCO    The Chinese are great gamblers. I knew one in medical school. He was killed in that Zeppelin crash. Do you ever gamble?

LIDUC    Never.

ROCCO    No. Well, Father LiDuc, I'm afraid this is the end of our relationship. I'm a busy man. I have to rely on first impressions. Obviously you have nothing to offer me.

LIDUC    I'm sorry. Perhaps your wife and I will find more in common.

ROCCO    Go easily with her. My wife is classically deluded. Are you familiar with *The Three Sisters* by Chekhov?

LIDUC  Of course.

ROCCO  My wife believes that she is a character from that play. Her namesake. The eldest sister.

LIDUC  How does she reconcile this belief with reality?

ROCCO  Which reality?

LIDUC  I understand.

ROCCO  Do you?

LIDUC  No.

ROCCO  No. The only way to understand it is to become part of it. I write letters. I send them to a friend in London. He posts them for me. She thinks they're from her sister. That's a secret. Do you like secrets?

LIDUC  No. But sometimes they're necessary.

ROCCO  Wisdom. Glib wisdom. But it's better than nothing. Maybe you'll save us all in spite of the odds.

LIDUC  I'm too young.

ROCCO  And I'm drunk. Tell my wife not to wait up. I have to disappear for a while.

[**ROCCO** *starts off taking the bottle with him*]

LIDUC  May I ask where to?

ROCCO  No! Yes. I'm having an illicit affair with a leopard. Three trees due east of the quagmire. Beware the cobra. Ask for Zelda.

[**ROCCO** *leaves.* **LIDUC** *sits. Closes his eyes. Leans back. The sound of an approaching automobile. Screeches to a halt. Door opens. Door slams shut. Footsteps. Eventually* **RITA** *appears. She is wearing a decorated bathrobe*]

RITA  The new priest.

LIDUC  Yes.

RITA  You don't look Chinese. They told me you were Chinese.

LIDUC  Who told you?

RITA  Them. The guys in the bushes.

[**LIDUC** *looks around nervously*]

Don't worry. They're harmless. They just follow me around 'cause they haven't got anything better to do.

[*Muttering from the bushes. She turns*]

You guys are getting pretty paranoid. You know that? Keep it down or you'll give yourselves a bad name. [*Silence*] Well, are you or aren't you?

LIDUC   What?

RITA   Chinese.

LIDUC   Half.

RITA   No kiddin'. Why are you shaking?

LIDUC   Nerves. This is my first mission. I mean I have —

RITA   Stage fright. Yeah. Where's the Doctor?

LIDUC   He went for a walk.

RITA   I'll bet he did.

LIDUC   I don't like the innuendo. Say what you mean.

RITA   Forget it. [*Hands* LIDUC *a wad of bills*] Here. Give him this for me, will ya. Tell him I don't need the action. Tell him he's worse than shit. Never mind. Just give him the money. I'll tell him he's worse than shit myself next time I see him.

LIDUC   All right.

RITA   Do you like my bathrobe? I painted it myself. Do you like the glitter?

LIDUC   It's very...

RITA   Crass. Yeah. It's crass. But I had no choice. It was either do it up vulgar or blend in with the scenery. I mean everyone else is so weird you know. Well, I was the last one to get here and all the other styles were taken. So I got left with 'vulgar.'

LIDUC   That's too bad.

RITA   I'm getting used to it. Yeah. You know, I was thinking about that on the way over. I haven't got much to do while I'm waiting for Chad so sometimes I just think. I was thinking how much I've come to like this place. It used to bore the bejesus outa me. But now, well, I guess it's just been a good change of pace for me. Like I'm on top of things. And back home it was always things being on top of me. Not that the money wasn't good. But the hours were lousy and my body was taking a real beating. And my flicks weren't good enough to be considered art so I was getting to feel kinda cheap. You know what this place is? I just thought of this. This place is my virgin father, Father. The one we all want.

LIDUC   I've never heard of anyone wanting a Virgin Father before. That's interesting.

RITA   Nah. It's hype. But at least it matches my clothes. Gotta run. [*Starts off*]

LIDUC   Bye-bye.

RITA    Wait. [*Stops*] You must have testicles. You know that? Staying here after what's happened. I mean Father Ricci was just a nosy son of a bitch and that one before him. Father whats-his-face.

LIDUC   Carson.

RITA    Yeah. He was a meddling mother too. But you seem different. You got testicles. And you look like the kinda man who'll mind his own business.

LIDUC   Is that a suggestion?

RITA    Could be. Gotta run. [*Starts off. Stops*] Oh, tell the Doc I understand, but that maybe some other people won't.

LIDUC   And what does that mean?

RITA    Don't worry about what it means. Just tell him. Bye for now.

LIDUC   And who can I say was calling?

RITA    [*leaving*] Just tell him Rita was here.
        [*Laughs. Leaves, humming 'Heat Wave.' LIDUC waves. Notices that his hand is trembling. Produces an envelope from a pocket. Sits on the steps. Pours some powder from it on to the back of his hand. Sniffs it. Closes his eyes. Sways gently for a while*]

LIDUC   Personality is a dangerous illusion. [*Falls back on the porch*]

[*Blackout*]
[*And the sound of some strange people in the distance singing 'Stand up for Jesus'*]

## Scene 5

*Late evening paranoia. We hear the* **CORPORAL** *laughing. Lights come up. The* **CORPORAL** *is startled and frightened. He staggers back. Sits, staring at us in fear.* **LIDUC** *is sitting on the picnic table, underlining passages in his Bible.* **OLGA** *comes briskly through the door, fresh and bright, carrying a parasol and a book.*

OLGA     I've decided to make a comeback. First things first. I'm going for a walk.

     *[Down the steps. Several confident steps straight ahead. Stops. Turns. A few paces to the left. Stops. Turns. Looks right]*
It's all the same. Foreign. Uninviting. Blandness in one direction. Danger in the other. Why bother choosing.

     *[Returns to her chair on the porch] [To no one in particular]* It's like this I think. One cannot afford to be a romantic. In this time. At this place. It's just too dangerous. Emotion is apt to be mistaken for weakness and weakness as an invitation to manipulate. *[Pause]* Yes. Good. I am thinking again. I'm going to be all right. *[Sits]* Good morning.

LIDUC     Good morning.

CORPORAL     *[directly outward]* And further more! *[Looks around. Whimpers]* Where was I?

LIDUC     You were describing the murders in all their gory detail.

CORPORAL     Yeah. Yeah, right. Are you feeling better? Not gonna vomit after all, eh?

LIDUC     No.

CORPORAL     Okay. Post scriptum to all that. *[With great emphasis and delight]* Both victims were found without clothing. Conclusion. The murderer has a fetish or two. Even Ricci's various pieces and parts were all found unclad. This brings into question sexual abuse, homosexuality, sodomy, obscene sexual abuse and necrophobia! *[Falls to his knees]*

OLGA     *[writhing from his descriptions]* Lunch!

LIDUC     Necrophilia.

CORPORAL     Yeah. Right.

OLGA     *[recovering]* Lunch?

LIDUC     I haven't had breakfast yet.

OLGA    Good idea. Neither have I. Tomas!

     [**LIDUC** *begins to underline in his Bible again.* **CORPORAL** *recovers. Closes in on* **LIDUC**]

CORPORAL    Do I have your undivided attention, Father?

LIDUC    Not really.

CORPORAL    Why not!?

LIDUC    [*nervously*] You see, Doctor and Mrs. Rocco are allowing me to give my lessons here. I've called the first one for this afternoon. And I'm not very well prepared. Perhaps we could talk later.

CORPORAL    Whatya mean later, man. You might not last the day.

OLGA    Tomas!

CORPORAL    Will you shut up!

OLGA    Shut up yourself, Lance! This is my house!

CORPORAL    So what!

     [**CORPORAL** *and* **OLGA** *stare at each other until* **LIDUC** *is overtaken by the silence*]

LIDUC    All right Corporal. Out with it. All this talk was in order to frighten me into doing what?

CORPORAL    Nothing. Don't go anywhere. And don't do nothin'. Just stay here where you're safe. I've got my hands full. There's rebellion in the air and we're surrounded by unpredictable primitives. And I don't need another dead priest. [*Grabs* **LIDUC***'s ears*] Do you understand me?

LIDUC    Yes.

CORPORAL    [*shaking* **LIDUC**] I hope so. I hope so, Mister. 'Cause if I catch you out running around unprotected I'm going to have to toss your ass in jail. And you know what that means. That means embarrassment. For both of us. Do you understand me?

LIDUC    [*crying*] I said yes.

CORPORAL    Okay. Okay. [*To* **OLGA**] Call me on the radio at the first sign of trouble.

OLGA    Of course.

CORPORAL    [*to* **LIDUC**. *Pointing a finger*] Okay. [**CORPORAL** *leaves*]

OLGA    He's worried about his job.

LIDUC    He's a fascist.

OLGA    Oh. You don't care much for fascists.

LIDUC    Who does?

OLGA    Other fascists, I suppose. [*Pause*] I mean they're still human beings, aren't they? Aren't they?

[**TOMAS** *comes out. Dressed in wonderful and fancy new clothes, strutting, smiling*]

Tomas. You are getting arrogant. In the future when I call you, come out immediately and humbly like the lackey you really are. Now go prepare tea and heat the croissants. We are breakfasting en retard upon the terrace.

**TOMAS**   Kali thiaskéthasi.

**OLGA**   Just get the tea.

[**TOMAS** *nods. Hands* **OLGA** *a letter. Goes back into the house*]

**LIDUC**   Where did he get the clothes?

**OLGA**   I don't know. He just came home one day wearing them. And he had an entire new wardrobe as well. I don't know where he got the money.

**LIDUC**   Why don't you ask him?

**OLGA**   Enrico doesn't allow me to say anything to him except to give him the simplest domestic commands. He says it might cause a haemorrhage. You see we found him in the desert surrounded by a platoon of dead soldiers. He was wearing an apron. And he had a bullet in his brain. It was like a Godsend to both of us. I needed a servant and Enrico needed somone on whom to test this new neuro-surgical procedure.

**LIDUC**   Which procedure is this?

**OLGA**   I can't tell you. It's illegal.

**LIDUC**   I was afraid it might be.

**OLGA**   It's a secret. All right?

**LIDUC**   I'll have to think about it.

**OLGA**   Oh no. I only told you because I thought I could trust you. If anyone finds out they'll send Enrico away and I'll have to go too. And I have a feeling I wouldn't much like it out there.

**LIDUC**   Out where?

**OLGA**   Anywhere.

**LIDUC**   All right. I won't tell anyone.

**OLGA**   Good.

**LIDUC**   I hope so. [*Pause*]

**OLGA**   Another letter from Masha. My sister. A good creature with an unfortunate past.

**LIDUC**   I know.

OLGA   What's that?

LIDUC   Nothing. Your sister. Is she your only relative?

OLGA   No. I have another sister. But she's too young and happy to be of any importance. And I had a brother too. But that's a long story.

LIDUC   Olga. [*He goes to her. Touches her shoulder*] I think I can help you.
[*She reacts violently. Pushes him away*]

OLGA   What nonsense is that. I don't need any help. I gave myself to Christ back in Russia and he promised he would take care of me. But if you have any spare time on your hands, I mean when you're not teaching the native people, you might see what you can do for my husband. He's 'haunted.' And Lance. He's 'haunted' too.

LIDUC   The Corporal's 'haunted'? How do you know?

OLGA   We had a brief affair. Enrico said he wouldn't mind as long as I didn't enjoy it too much. It was in the middle of the monsoon season. I became restless. [*Sighs*] It's all right. I confessed to Father Ricci and he beat me unconscious to help me repent. [*Sighs again*] Anyway Lance talks in his sleep. I found out that he was drummed out of the R.C.M.P. for shooting a farmer's cows. It seems that the expression in their eyes made him feel they were in 'eternal misery.' He can't stand seeing 'eternal misery.' He calls it 'evil whining misery.' Under all that bravado, he's really just a frightened boy.

LIDUC   [*looks around. Sits*] Does he still kill things that he thinks are in eternal misery?

OLGA   I don't know. That's a good question. You should ask him. But be careful how you do it. Because he's 'haunted.' Why are you shaking?
[**LIDUC** *takes out his envelope. Sniffs some of his powder*]
What's that?

LIDUC   A dangerous drug.

OLGA   [*backs away*] How nice. You know I wonder if our conversation has been good for me. It seems I decided to forget all these things a while ago. Of course I can't forget my family because Masha keeps writing me these damn letters. But I do try and forget about Lance. And especially my husband.

LIDUC     I'm sorry. I thought some information about everyone might help me adjust.

OLGA     Well. We're simple people, really.

> [**TOMAS** *brings out the tea and biscuits on a tray. Sets them down on a small table near* **OLGA**'s *chair*]

Change your bandage, Tomas. You're bleeding on the croissants.

> [**TOMAS** *touches his head. Frowns. Goes back inside*]

Tell me about yourself. Tell me about your family. I just love hearing about families.

LIDUC     Well ...

OLGA     No. Please. It helps me. You said you wanted to help me.

LIDUC     You said you didn't need help.

OLGA     Well, I expected you to see that I was lying. Tell me. Please. Especially about your problems. Hearing about other people's problems some how comforts me. [*A disturbing smile*] Please!

> [**LIDUC** *stands.*

LIDUC     My father was Chinese. My mother was a Jew. They were both incurably insane by the time I was ten. Some say they drove each other mad. Others say it was a bizarre game of one-upmanship. I was taken by the only relative I had. An uncle who was a convert to Catholicism. He was a fanatic. He died and I was put in the custody of the Church. That was twelve years ago. I just got out last month. I am a neurotic who is also like you say 'haunted.' And I developed several habits along the way through my education. Among them, a desire for the bodies of lean young men, and an attraction to the joys of several drugs. The more dangerous the better. I am a potential source of deep embarrassment to the Church. Which is why I was sent here. This is where priests like myself and Father Ricci, who was an infamous sadist by the way, are sent in the hope that they will never be heard of again. So far a perfect record. Why is your mouth hanging open?

OLGA     Would you like some tea?

LIDUC     [*only now does he become mobile*] But the strangest thing. In the middle of all that and even now, my occasional relapse into total catatonia notwithstanding, I still have a relationship with God. I love him. And I trust him. And until I am done away with I will

endeavour to bring him and his word to others. All I need now is
a congregation. Do you think they'll come? If I wait long enough
they will. They must.

OLGA  Father. Would you like some tea?

LIDUC  [*smiles*] Yes. I feel good. Thank you for the opportunity to speak.
Yes I will have some tea. [*Goes to get himself some*] And what
about you? Has hearing all this helped you? God is a reality, you
know. He's better than even the best illusions.

OLGA  Maybe. But he's not so accessible.

[**ROCCO** *comes out, in an undershirt. He is hung over*]

LIDUC  Good morning.

ROCCO  Liar. Don't you know that the sun is slowly dying. How can
there be any *good* mornings? Where's your compassion? Ah,
what a bunch of shit. Who wants to hear that shit. This isn't Italy.
And I am no longer young enough to call out my reserves and
hope for the best.

OLGA  Is your work going badly? [*To* LIDUC] His work is his life.

ROCCO  The freighter of my existence has struck a reef and all my
chattels are getting wet.

[**LIDUC** *reaches into his pocket. Produces the money. Hands it
to* **ROCCO**]

LIDUC  From the lady called Rita.

ROCCO  Excuse me. No. Don't. Who cares. [*Starts back inside*]

OLGA  [*to* LIDUC] He's trying to forget. He spends a lot of time trying to
forget.

ROCCO  [*turning around*] Shut up. Hear it?

OLGA  What? [*Pulls a small pistol from her skirt*]

LIDUC  Why do you carry a gun?

OLGA  Self protection. We're surrounded by unhealthy people You and I
are the only ones around here who aren't paranoid.

ROCCO  Shush. Hear it?

OLGA  What?!

ROCCO  Hear it now?

OLGA  No.

ROCCO  Hit the dirt!

[*They all duck. After a moment* **ROCCO** *stands. Looks through
the open door into the house. The other two join him*]

OLGA  What was it?

[**ROCCO** *scratches his head. Looks around. Tucks in his undershirt. Makes a meaningless gesture. Looks around. Smiles. Scratches his head*]

ROCCO    Poison dart.

[*They all start slowly into the house, looking around cautiously.* **OLGA** *and* **ROCCO** *go inside.* **LIDUC** *changes his mind. Comes back down the steps. Looks around. Opens up his arms*]

LIDUC    I have nothing to hide. In spite of everything I am still innocent.

[*Hears something. Whimpers. Puts his hands above his head*]

[*Blackout*]
[*Drums, muffled and slow*]

# Scene 6

*The drums become gradually more distinct. Then they fade in
and out throughout the scene. Evening.* LIDUC *is still waiting
with open arms. He moves only his eyes, which dash about in
reaction to various noises from the bushes. Talking. Muttering.
Footsteps. Branches breaking. Muffled screams. Complaints.
Garbage cans banging. Babies crying. Birds screeching. And
every once in a while a shot. A moan. And an explosion or two in
the distance. And the sound of grass burning. Through all this*
LIDUC *waits, moving only his eyes. Finally ...*

OLGA  [*voice from inside the house*] No. Keep them out of my house.
ROCCO  [*voice from inside the house*] What are you doing?
OLGA  [*from inside*] Keep away.
ROCCO  [*voice*] Give it back.
OLGA  [*voice*] Keep away.
ROCCO  [*voice*] Don't do it.
OLGA  [*voice*] Damn you! Damn you!
ROCCO  [*voice*] No! Don't!
[*The sound of a bottle crashing*]
[*voice*] Oh my God. My work. My work.
OLGA  [*voice*] Out of my house.
[*She comes hysterically through the door, covered with blood,
her hands full of human organs, intestines and things.* LIDUC
*turns away in disgust, starts to wander aimlessly around.*
OLGA *throws them down on the ground. Picks them up.
Throws them toward us. They don't go very far so she kicks
them some more, closer to us, then closer.* ROCCO *comes out,
in a rage, carrying a piece of intestine*]
ROCCO  Stupid woman. Goddamn lunatic. You've ruined my work. No
brains, woman. You've got mush for brains.
OLGA  You brought them into my house. You put them on my dresser.
ROCCO  Jesus. Simple Jesus. It wasn't me. It must have been Tomas.
OLGA  I don't care. I saw them. I never wanted to see them. You're sick
and evil and you let me see them. Damn you anyway. Damn
you.

ROCCO    Shut up. [*Looks at his piece of intestine*] What did you do with the rest?

OLGA    Into the swamp. Threw it away. Threw it away.

ROCCO    That was Old Peter. You threw away Old Peter. This is all that's left.

OLGA    Oh my God.

ROCCO    I taught that man how to play chess. It took me two years. Because he was a dumb native. Two wasted years reclaimed for my experiments. And you've thrown him into the bushes to rot away uselessly.

OLGA    You're a butcher.

ROCCO    I'm a scientist.

OLGA    Scientists experiment with pigs.

ROCCO    What a bunch of shit. Even a child could tell you that you don't experiment with pigs to find out what's wrong with people.

OLGA    You've lost your mind. It's for nothing. They'll look up your war record and put you in prison forever. It's all for nothing.

ROCCO    It's for my work. I will find the cure to end all cures. No matter what it is. Or even that I do not know what it is. And even if I never find it, I'm safe. Safe. Safe. In the bowels of the earth. Because there's something about committing crimes against humanity that puts you in touch with the purpose of the universe.

LIDUC    That is the most intellectually obscene comment I have ever heard.

OLGA    [*hears something inside the house*] What's that?
         [*Starts inside in a daze muttering 'Oh no, oh no.'*]

LIDUC    God have mercy on the feeble, the diseased and the deluded.

ROCCO    Woman! You will mean nothing to me in the end. I am a scientist. And you are just a diversion. [*To the intestines*] I'm sorry Old Peter. This is the truth. Just between you and me. It's not glory I'm after. It's redemption.
         [**LIDUC** *utters a sentence in Chinese directed at the doctor's condition*]
         Nonsense. I am safe. I am sinking with confidence into the mire. It's all out in the open and I'm safer than ever. I have finally destroyed that fucking tower and now there are only three forces

in the world. God. Ignorance. And me.

[OLGA *screams inside the house. More a cry of anguish than a scream, actually*]

LIDUC    Doctor, your soul is in serious trouble.

[OLGA *runs out of the house carrying a picture frame*]

OLGA    We've been robbed. They've taken my Renoir. In retribution for your crimes. You've capsized me.

ROCCO    My notebooks! [*He runs into the house*]

OLGA    My Renoir. My Renoir. My sanity.

LIDUC    [*takes out his cocaine*] Have some of this.

OLGA    No.

LIDUC    Please, a touch of oblivion will settle you down.

OLGA    No. I prefer to have a dream. Yes. I'm going to go inside. Lie down. And have a dream. A very vivid one. About the Victoria and Albert museum. Yes. [*Stands*] Masha will meet me at the station. [*Starts inside*] Sloan Square. South Kensington. Gloucester Road.

[*She disappears into the house*]

LIDUC    [*sits. Sniffs some powder. Looks up*] I don't like the odds. [*Sniffs some more*] But I will not give up.

[ROCCO *comes out*]

ROCCO    My notebooks. My experiments. Gone. All gone. My safety is on the way. Now only to wait for the cataclysm.

[ROCCO *lies down on the operating table. The drums get a bit louder.* LIDUC *looks around. Looks at* ROCCO. *Chuckles. Goes and sits on the picnic table.* TOMAS *comes out of the bushes counting money, wearing a new suit, smoking a cigar. Sees the doctor. Pulls a knife. Sneaks up toward him. His head is larger and more blood is showing on his bandage*]

LIDUC    Be careful, doctor. Behind you.

[ROCCO *sits up.* TOMAS *puts on a look of surprise*]

ROCCO    What were you doing?

TOMAS    Mistake.

ROCCO    Go inside. Have a bath. Have two baths. Then crawl into bed with my wife. She's a bit frustrated. She needs sex. And I have other things on my mind. Inside. My wife. Sex. Understand?

TOMAS    Yais. Sex. You come too.

ROCCO   [*looks at him oddly*] No. [*Lies down again*]
          [**TOMAS** *starts inside. Stops. Goes to* **LIDUC***. Sizes him up.*
          *Musses his hair*]
TOMAS   You come too?
LIDUC   Maybe later.
          [**TOMAS** *laughs. Goes inside.* **LIDUC** *looks out at us*]
          Clever. Clever. [*Shaking a finger*] But I'm not going to be led into
          temptation. You naughty God you. [*Laughs*]
          [*We hear* **RITA** *approaching through the jungle, cursing to*
          *herself.* **LIDUC** *produces a bottle of pills from his coat pocket.*
          *Pops a couple. Laughs.* **RITA** *comes on, her bathrobe torn,*
          *black underwear beneath it, her face a bit soiled, muttering,*
          *walking oddly*]
RITA    Those fuckers. Those mothers. Those lousy scumbags. Jesus. It's
          a double cross. Screwed on all sides. Where's Tomas?
ROCCO   Busy. Come back later.
RITA    He's done me in. He took their money and bought himself
          clothes. Fucking suits and ties and shoes. Clothes.
LIDUC   What was he supposed to buy?
RITA    Guns.
LIDUC   What for?
RITA    I don't know what for. For some stupid uprising, I guess. I don't
          know. And I don't care. I needed the money. The money.
LIDUC   I'm sorry for you.
RITA    What's that?
LIDUC   I'm sorry for you.
RITA    Oh you are. Why?
LIDUC   Because you're dumb. Because you've been exploited. Ex-
          ploited by people who you were trying to exploit. And that's sad.
          Jesus doesn't mind losers but he has no patience for idiots.
RITA    They raped me.
LIDUC   Did you enjoy it?
RITA    Hey come on. Even Father Ricci never asked questions like that.
          You're weird.
LIDUC   True.
RITA    [*sits down on the steps. Pause*] I was caught off guard. Leaning
          against my tree. Sipping Southern Comfort. Looking north to-
          ward the high grass. Thinking everything was fine. Counting

money in my head. Figuring we had enough for a month's shooting. Thinking how sorry Chad was every time he beat me up and how sorry I was for calling the police that last time. And how sincere Chad looked when he came into my hospital room with those cops. Leaning against that tree with the flies in my ears. Getting really very deeply into Susan Hayward in the Snows of Kilimanjaro.

[*Drums start. Louder*]

And then they were on me with their funny talk and their wiped out eyes and their hands smeared with elephant fat. Sticking their long dry dongs in me. And all the time asking where their money was and telling me how they'd had to get that money by cashing in empty soda bottles and stealing hub caps and costume jewellery from all the white trash and that they were really pissed off that they didn't have any guns to blow everyone's head off and set up a new republic dedicated to socialistic democracy and put the white European honkey trash in little boxes with bars on them and feed them gruel and hit their hands with long sticks. [*Drums stop. Pause*] But through all that I was fine. I was all right. Because I kept telling myself it wasn't real. Nobody rapes me. Nobody ever raped Susan Hayward or Rita Hayworth. And nobody rapes me. But, Jesus, they said that if they didn't get their money or their guns pretty damn soon they were gonna do it again. Only this time torture me and take pictures of my mutilated body and send them to all those cheap tabloids back home. That's when I passed out. Because the idea of being on the front cover of one of those things lying there like a matted rug just ran like vomit all through my body and my mind. And I passed out.

[*A scream from the house.* **TOMAS** *runs out. Putting on his undershorts*]

[*To* **TOMAS**] And it's your fault, you mother.

[*She steps toward* **TOMAS**. *He runs away. Before he disappears into the bushes,* **RITA** *produces a pistol from her bathrobe* — *points it at* **TOMAS'** *back. But does not shoot.* **TOMAS** *is gone.* **RITA** *drops the gun*]

I couldn't. He's still my only friend.

[*A gun shot from inside the house.* **ROCCO** *sits up*]

ROCCO     She's shot herself.

       [**ROCCO** *and* **LIDUC** *rush toward the door.* **ROCCO** *goes in.*
       **LIDUC** *stops. Returns for his Bible. Gets it. Runs in*]

RITA     Sometimes I just feel like giving up.

       [*Pause.* **TOMAS** *comes running on. Disappears into the bushes
       on the other side of the house. The* **CORPORAL** *comes running
       on. He is delirious and sweating profusely*]

CORPORAL     Did you see him?

RITA     A total blur.

CORPORAL     A subversive. One of many. They're all over the place. Getting
ready to attack. I've got an informant. He tells me they've got a
new leader and a real sharpy he's supposed to be too. He's
organized them and they're ready to move.

RITA     You're sweating like a pig.

CORPORAL     Fever. Malaria.

       [*Drums start again. Producing a nylon stocking. turning
       around feverishly*]

Here we go. They followed me. It's all over.

       [*Approaching* **RITA** *slowly*]

Listen I know you're in with them. Use your influence. It's me
they want. They know I've been doing you-know-what with all
their eleven-year-old daughters. Old Joseph's eleven- year-old
daughter in particular. It was good. We both liked it. But she
went funny. Stole my pistol and tried to shoot off my you-
know-what. I liked that too. But then she started to cry and her
eyes got all spongy and I knew she was in 'misery.' 'Evil whining
misery.'

RITA     You killed that little girl!

CORPORAL     Shut up. It's a secret.

       [*The* **CORPORAL** *puts the stocking around* **RITA**'*s neck.* **RITA**
       *is gagging.* **CORPORAL** *is squeezing.* **LIDUC** *comes out*]

LIDUC     Olga has shot herself in the chest. Can we divert ourselves for a
moment to pray for her.

       [**CORPORAL** *drops* **RITA**. *Turns on* **LIDUC**]

CORPORAL     Shut up. You smell. I saw what you've got written on the inside
cover of your Bible. 'Prophecy is an escape from memory.' Now
what in the hell does that mean?

[*Raises the stocking and lunges at* **LIDUC**. **LIDUC** *ducks. Runs back inside.* **RITA** *has crawled to a chair.* **CORPORAL** *is strangling himself*]

It means misery! Misery in the mind. Everyone's got it and everyone has to be put put of it. [*Thinks. Drops stocking*] But not me. I gotta live. [*Grabs* **RITA**. *Lifts her in a bear hug*] Help me.

RITA    No.

CORPORAL    I gotta live. Gotta overcome the disgrace of being drummed outa the Mounties. My father was a policeman.

RITA    Cut the crap. And let me go.

CORPORAL    My father was a bull. Deep murky brown eyes. Lips like pancakes. We called him Sarge.

RITA    Let me go, you goddamn oaf.
[*Drums stop.* **CORPORAL** *drops* **RITA**. *Looks around in a panic*]

CORPORAL    What's going on here?

RITA    It's a power struggle.
[*Pause*]

CORPORAL    Yeah. That's it. Between who?

RITA    You and me.

CORPORAL    Yeah. Who's winning?

RITA    I am.

CORPORAL    [*slaps her*] Who's winning now?

RITA    I am.

CORPORAL    [*slaps her*] And who's winning now?

RITA    [*knees him in the groin. He falls to his knees*] I am.

CORPORAL    Don't look at me like that, eh. I know what you're thinking.

RITA    I'm thinking how silly you look. Just like my man looked when I hit him with my cast in that hospital room.
[*The* **CORPORAL** *is crawling away from her*]

CORPORAL    You're passing judgement on me. In times of crisis there are only two kinds of people. People who behave badly and people who pass judgement on the people who behave badly. And you're one of them. Just like my father. He's dead. But he never lets me forget.
[**CORPORAL** *collapses. Face down.* **LIDUC** *comes out. Carrying his valise*]

LIDUC    What's wrong with him?

RITA   He's delirious.

[*Suddenly the* **CORPORAL** *gets to his knees. Draws his gun*]

CORPORAL   I know what they want. I know what they all want. They want to be put outa their misery. And maybe they want a little sexual abuse too. Oh, and I'm just the man to give it to them. [*Gets to his feet*] All right. All right. [*Staggers off*]

[**ROCCO** *comes out of the house*]

ROCCO   I've decided that I want to live. [*Talking to us*] I'll do anything you want. Just let me get on with my work. My work is my penance. And my penance is everything. [*To* LIDUC] You. Priest. Go see if you can make them understand.

[*But* **LIDUC** *has taken the materials of a heroin user out of his valise. And is in the process of shooting up*]

LIDUC   Okay. Sure. But first I have to get closer to God. I have the feeling we've been out of touch.

RITA   Don't let them take any pictures of my mutilated body.

ROCCO   Be quiet. I'm preparing myself to beg.

[**OLGA** *comes out of the house. Carrying her picture frame. Her chest wrapped in bandages*]

OLGA   Oh, hello Shirley.

RITA   The name's Rita.

OLGA   Your name is Shirley Morgan. But not to worry. Our secret. [*Groans*] Enrico. I have a complaint to make about that animal you sent into my bed. His erection was monumental but his manner was disgusting. He took me in the rectum. Good taste died immediately. And I have decided to follow. [*Pause*] To die. On my way to Moscow. Finally leaving. Finally getting there. Finally. Moscow. [*Giggles*] Ah. What a bad joke it really is.

[*A scream from the jungle*]

Bravo. [*She dies, leaning against a post on the porch*]

RITA   Is she dead?

ROCCO   I guess so.

LIDUC   I can cope. No. I can't cope.

RITA   Well if it's gonna happen I wanna look my best. Or else everyone will just look at my picture and say, 'She was a cheap porno queen and she died looking like one.' And no one will ever believe that I had what I had beneath all this shit. And the world won't be able to remember me with love.

[*She takes a small compact and lipstick from her pocket. Begins to apply the lipstick.* **CORPORAL** *comes on. Minus one arm. Blood dripping. A note attached to his sleeve. The note is plainly visible. A child's handwriting. It reads, 'Entertain us.'*]
Your arm.

CORPORAL   Where is it?

RITA   I don't know.

CORPORAL   Then it's gone. They really took it off. Failed again. [*Looks up*] Sorry Sarge.

ROCCO   That note on his sleeve.
      [**RITA** *goes to get it*]

LIDUC   [*chuckles. Looks up*] Amazing. I don't understand how you make all this violence seem so gratuitous.

ROCCO   What's it say? I'll do anything it says.

RITA   [*reads*] 'Entertain us.' [*Pause. They all look around. And from this moment there is a distinct tendency for everyone to play outward*]

ROCCO   [*pacing*] Entertain them? Entertain them.

RITA   How?

ROCCO   I'm thinking.

CORPORAL   I'm bleeding to death!
      [*He begins to cry*]

ROCCO   Then do it quietly. I'm thinking.

RITA   [*beginning to disrobe*] I won't do anything disgusting. I'll entertain but I won't be cheap.

ROCCO   You'll do what I tell you. Or I'll slit your throat.

RITA   Hey. We're friends.
      [*She crumbles onto the steps*]

ROCCO   I want to live.

LIDUC   Excuse me. But what for?

ROCCO   You give me a reason.

LIDUC   To save humanity.
      [*Whistles in self-approval*]

ROCCO   Corporal. Shut-up. You're whining.
      [*The* **CORPORAL** *has been writhing on the ground*]

CORPORAL   Whining? [*Sits up*] Oh my God. I'm whining. Evil whining? [*Wraps his one arm around* **ROCCO**'s *leg*] Oh doctor, you gotta put me outta my misery.
      [**ROCCO** *shakes him loose*]

ROCCO    No. You'll live. Till I'm safe. You'll bleed till I'm safe. All of
         you. We'll all entertain together. No one gets safe before me.
LIDUC    [*points to* OLGA] Except her.
         [ROCCO *grabs* RITA's *lipstick. Goes to* OLGA]
ROCCO    No. Not even her.
         [*The* CORPORAL *is crawling toward us. Looking along the
         ground. Smiling insanely*]
CORPORAL Ants. Huge red ants. They've smelled my blood. And they've
         come to nibble on my stump.
         [ROCCO *is using the lipstick to paint* OLGA's *face: two tears
         and a huge obscene smile.* TOMAS *comes out of the jungle
         wearing priest's clothes, two crosses around his neck, carrying
         a spear and an enormous wad of money*]
LIDUC    [*giddily*] Look at him. Where'd you get those clothes?
TOMAS    God.
LIDUC    Where'd you get those two crucifixes?
TOMAS    God. [LIDUC *has one moment of unbridled passion in this play.
         He stands. And projects*]
LIDUC    Liar!! [TOMAS *attacks him. Pushes him down. Leans over. mass-
         ages his crotch. Whispers something terrible in his ear*]
         [*Trembling*] It's true. Oh my God. It's true.
         [TOMAS *laughs maniacally. Screams. Throws the money up
         and all over the ground*]
ROCCO    I've got it! Hum. [*Goes to Rita*] Everyone hum!
RITA     [*singing*] 'We're having a heat wave ...'
ROCCO    No. Something Russian. [ROCCO *starts to hum 'Swan Lake'.*
         RITA *joins in.* ROCCO *goes to* LIDUC. *Drags him up. Gets* LIDUC
         *to join in. The* CORPORAL *is hearing humming noises*]
CORPORAL Locusts! Enormous pecking locusts!
         [ROCCO *is now standing over* CORPORAL. *Pulling his hair*]
ROCCO    Hum!
         [*Everyone is humming or singing 'Swan Lake', staring hard at
         us and singing with increasing concern, getting louder and
         louder.* ROCCO *goes to* OLGA. *Drags her to a chair. Puts her
         on his knee. Sticks his hand up the back of her dress to her
         throat. And as* Swan Lake *approaches a crescendo it is
         interrupted by a bizarre scream from* OLGA's *throat. Silence.*
         ROCCO *is manipulating* OLGA's *vocal chords, her head flop-*

*ping lifelessly around until his is able to position her properly.*
*He clears his throat. Moves* **OLGA**'s *jaw. And the following*
*speech comes from* **OLGA**, *in her own voice, but distorted and*
*unbearably erratic.* **ROCCO** *silently mouths the words of*
**OLGA**'s *final speech:*]

OLGA   'The music is so gay, so confident. And one longs for life! Oh,
my God! Time will pass, and we shall go away forever, and we
shall be forgotten, our faces will be forgotten, our voices and
how many there were of us. But our sufferings will pass into joy
for those who will live after us, happiness and peace will be
established upon earth and they will remember kindly and bless
those who have lived before. Oh dear sisters our life is not ended
yet. We shall live! The music is so gay, so joyful, and it seems as
though a little more and we shall know what we are living for,
why we are suffering ... oh. If only we could know. If only we
could know!!'

[*And* **OLGA**'s *mouth is still moving as if there were more to say.*
*But all we hear are groans and mutterings.* **ROCCO** *is smiling*
*at us obsequiously. The others are staring at disbelief at* **OLGA**.
**TOMAS** *looks at them. At us. Raises his arm and beckons. The*
*drums explode. Sudden violence and activity from the bushes,*
*getting closer and louder. Everyone on their feet now, edging*
*toward the door of the house, looking at us in confusion and*
*growing anxiety — backing up slowly*]

[*Blackout*]


THE END

GEORGE F. WALKER'S

# RAMONA AND THE WHITE SLAVES

'An exotic, beguiling play'

Directed by GEORGE F. WALKER
Designed by SHAWN KERWIN

Starring DAVID BOLT, DORIS COWAN,
BARBARA GORDON, JIM HENSHAW
JEANNIE WALKER

PREVIEWS:
Jan. 6th to 8th ~ 99¢
OPENS:
Jan. 9th, 1976

Tuesday through Sunday 8:30 p.m.
Res. and Info.: 864-9971
207 Adelaide St. E. Toronto

The Year: 1919
The Place: The suburbs of Hong Kong

*Ramona and the White Slaves* was first produced at the Factory Theatre Lab with the following cast:

RAMONA MARIA DA COSTA     Barbara Gordon
COOK/SEBASTIAN     David Bolt
FRIEDRICH/MITCH     Jim Henshaw
LESLIE     Jeannie Walker
GLORIA     Doris Cowan

Set & costume designed by: Shawn Kerwin
Lighting designed by: Alan Richardson
Directed by: George F. Walker

*Persons*
RAMONA MARIA DA COSTA
GLORIA  (mid-twenties)
LESLIE  (about 17)
FRIEDRICH  (Mitch)
MR. SEBASTIAN  (*must* be played by
COOK     the same actor)

*Note:* 'There will be no intermission.'

# Scene 1

*Time is at play here. In her scenes with* **COOK**, **RAMONA** *should somehow look older (more disturbed) even though some of these scenes do not necessarily take place in the present — and not all of the scenes excluding* **COOK** *take place in the past.*

*The year is 1919 and we are in the suburbs of Hong Kong.*

## I

**COOK**. *In a trench coat. Below a gas burning street lamp.*

COOK   It's a dry hard night in the suburbs of Hong Kong. The world is no longer at war. Although some of the more critically wounded are still twitching in their hospital beds. But it's probably better that we forget about them. Hong Kong has more pressing problems. Foreigners are swarming into the city. The crime rate is rising. It's ninety-two degrees Farenheit. And Ramona Maria da Costa is having an opium nightmare. [*He takes out a cheroot. Lights it*] She is about to be raped by a poisonous lizard.
   [*Lights up on* **RAMONA** *in the smoke-filled bedroom. Sitting up in bed. Immobile. Eyes wide*]

RAMONA   It paces slowly back and forth across my bed. Inches away from the soles of my feet. Head cocked arrogantly. Silently hissing.

COOK   Your typical reptile.

RAMONA   Horny speckled lizard. Hissing. Drooling. Foot sucking. And that sickly lizard grin. As it stops its pacing and crawls beneath the sheets.
   [**COOK** *is referring to a notebook*]

COOK   Satin sheets. Imported. Expensive. Very difficult to get. Unless you are a person of means. Any means.

RAMONA   Closer. See the ugly little hump it makes between my legs. Little scratching feet. Closer. Beware the tongue. It's wet with awful poison. Closer. Oh, father think twice before you do. I'm just a little Catholic girl and I can't afford any more sins. Closer. Then at least turn off the light and we'll lie and listen first to make sure mother superior is fast asleep. Closer.
   [**RAMONA** *sighs. Closes her eyes. Lights out on the bedroom*]

COOK    Elsewhere, a few dozen children are safe from the menaces of sex and drugs.

      *[Drops his cheroot. Crushes it with his foot]*
So I hear.

*[Blackout]*

*Footsteps in the darkness. Lights up. Cook has just entered the bedroom and is leaning against the door.*

COOK    Much of the following borders on the truth. Ramona Maria da Costa was born in a small impoverished village near Lisbon. When she was sixteen she entered a convent. Time passed. Things occasionally happened. Then two months after taking her final vows she left the convent and Portugal in the company of a Father Miguel Barreno. Together they came to the Orient where they did the work of their church for over five years. During the sixth year they left their church and got married. Three months later Miguel Barreno was mysteriously killed. His body was shipped back to Portugal. Ramona Maria da Costa Barreno went with it. She was away from the Orient for a year. She travelled. Did certain things. And returned a different kind of woman. She does 'business' here now. Under the direction of a Mister H. T. Sebastian. Her 'business' is not legal but she has always been somehow beyond the reach of the law. Until now. Last night a man was killed beneath her bedroom window. *[Another cheroot]* I am in charge of detectives in the suburbs of Hong Kong.

*[Blackout]*

# Scene 2

*Taper-time.* **RAMONA** *is leaning against the edge of the open door.*
*Looking down the hall. Occasionally waving. Blowing a kiss. She*
*is wearing a simple silk bathrobe.*
**FRIEDRICH** *is sitting at the piano. Chin in hand. He is*
*fashionably dressed. Although his clothes are a bit too big.*
**LESLIE** *is sitting on the bed reading* **FRIEDRICH** *a story. She is*
*seventeen but could look younger. She is dressed in some kind of*
*school uniform. Black and white. Very neat. One of her hands is*
*hidden by a fur muffler.*

LESLIE 'The Chevalier Tannhauser, having lighted off his horse, stood
doubtfully for a moment beneath the ombre gateway of the
Venusberg, troubled with an exquisite fear lest a day's travel
should have too cruelly undone the laboured niceness of his
dress. His hand, slim and gracious as La Marquise du Deffand's
in the drawing by Carmontelle, played nervously about the gold
hair that fell upon his shoulder like a finely curled peruke, and
from point to point of a precise toilet – '

FRIEDRICH [*the proper pronunciation*] Toilet.

LESLIE 'And from point to point of a precise ... toilet ... the fingers
wandered, quelling the little mutinies of cravat and ruffle.'

FRIEDRICH [*from memory*] 'It was taper-time. When the earth puts on its
cloak of mists and shadows, when the enchanted woods are
stirred with light footfalls and slender voices of the fairies, when
all the air is full of delicate influences, and even the beaux,
seated at their dressing tables, dream a little.' [*He turns his head*
*slowly to* **LESLIE**] 'A delicious moment, thought Tannhauser, to
slip into exile.'

[*Pause.* **LESLIE** *purses her lip. Slams the book closed*]

FRIEDRICH Stylish, isn't it.

[**LESLIE** *shrugs.* **FRIEDRICH** *gestures for her to continue.*
**LESLIE** *ignores him*]

FRIEDRICH Come on, Leslie, read some more. Don't be such a snot.

[**LESLIE** *shakes her head.* **FRIEDRICH** *shrugs. Hits one note*
*on the piano.* **RAMONA** *is slightly startled*]

RAMONA   He's gone.
         [*She sighs loudly to gather their attention. Then closes the door*]

RAMONA   He's gone. I'll miss him. Yes I will. Until his boat comes again and I look down from my window to see him sliding and sweating down the gang plank. Wiping his forehead with that filthy handkerchief. His belly moving up and down like a sleeping cow. [*Smiles*] But. In the meantime. I'll miss him. My darling ...

LESLIE   Elliot.

FRIEDRICH [*whispering*] It was on the tip of her tongue.

RAMONA   Darling Elliot. Oh the poor man. It just occurred to me that the world is at war and that his boat might get lost at sea. Friedrich. Play something ironic for me.

FRIEDRICH I can't.

RAMONA   Then get out.
         [**RAMONA** *goes to the window.* **FRIEDRICH** *lowers himself from the piano stool on to a small wooden platform about two foot square. Which has rollers on each corner. He has no legs. His oversized top coat covers his stumps*]

LESLIE   Do you need any help?

FRIEDRICH No.
         [*He is rolling toward the door*]

RAMONA   Don't go far, sweet.

FRIEDRICH No mother.

RAMONA   I suggest you go to the bald-headed man's room.

FRIEDRICH For what purpose.

RAMONA   So that you can smoke some of his opium.

FRIEDRICH Why?

RAMONA   So that you can forget.

FRIEDRICH Forget what?

RAMONA   [*looks him over*] Don't be silly.
         [**FRIEDRICH** *shakes his head. Reaches for the door knob*]

RAMONA   Friedrich?

FRIEDRICH Yes?

RAMONA   Do you think you could do something about the squeak in your little wheels. It's just a touch unnerving.
         [**FRIEDRICH** *smiles strangely. Backs out. Closes door*]

RAMONA  [*more or less to herself*] Well if I don't tell him these things, who will. [*Looks toward door*] After all I am his ... [*Pause*] And he is my ... [*Turns toward window. Sighs*]

      [**LESLIE** *stands. Goes to Ramona's side*]

LESLIE  I need some money.

RAMONA  [*suddenly happy*] Have you ever noticed how you sometimes speak to me. Sometimes you speak to me like I'm your ... [*gestures vaguely*]

LESLIE  I need the money to buy new underwear.

RAMONA  Why don't you borrow your sister's underwear.

LESLIE  She's using it.

RAMONA  Sometimes I wish that you *were* my ... and that the bald-headed man was our wealthy but 'distant' relative. And that he loved us passionately, perhaps even perversely but discreetly and from a 'distance.' And that he sent us huge sums of money on a regular basis. In neat little piles of crisp new bills. [*Pats her on the head*] You know I don't have any money. I never have any money. You'll have to ask him for it and then bring him back the bill of sale. Just like always.

LESLIE  No. He won't give me any. Something about a deficit. What should I do.

RAMONA  Kill him.

      [*They look at each other.* **LESLIE** *appears shaken*]

RAMONA  [*smiles*] It was a joke.

LESLIE  Oh.

RAMONA  Look. An occurence down in the street. Two men conversing. At first calmly. Rationally. Then with strange gesticulations. One suddenly pulling a knife and stabbing the other in the stomach. The criminal escaping artfully through the disgusting masses of starving people. The victim lying twisted and bleeding in the street is our friend.

LESLIE  Which one?

RAMONA  The one who just left us. Dear sweet ...

LESLIE  [*she looks*] Elliot.

RAMONA  Yes. He's dying isn't he. See how the stomach slows its heaving. He's dying.

      [*pause*]

LESLIE  He's dead.

RAMONA     Quickly. Get down there without being seen. There's a plain brown envelope in his breast pocket on the right side. Bring it to me.

      [LESLIE *starts off slowly*]

RAMONA     Quickly. Before the cannibals take his body.

LESLIE     The what?

RAMONA     Also. Send your sister to me.

LESLIE     But they just let her out of the cellar this morning. She's sleeping.

RAMONA     Wake her. [*claps her hands*] Quickly.

      [LESLIE *leaves.* RAMONA *goes to the window again. Smiles. Then suddenly her expression changes*]

RAMONA     Get away from that body you people. Get away. [*She grabs something as if to throw it out*] Don't touch it. Get away. You demented heathens. Get away from there. [*grabs something else*] The Christian god is watching you. Get away. Get ... [*is about to throw both objects but stops*] That's better. [*Smiles. Puts objects back. To herself*] The Christian god [*Chuckles. Crosses herself four or five times really fast. Laughs*] The Christian god is watching you. Oh yes. [*Giggles. Runs one hand through her hair*] I really must watch my language. [*sighs*]

      [GLORIA *comes in. Same kind of uniform as* LESLIE'*s but hers is ripped and soiled. She looks at* RAMONA. *Flops into one of the chairs. Legs outstretched. Apparently a lethargic person. A moment's silence as they look each other over*]

RAMONA     Did you have a nice sleep.

GLORIA     Terrific. What do you want.

      [RAMONA *goes to her dressing table. Sits. Begins to brush her hair*]

RAMONA     Money. Adventure. Pretty things.

GLORIA     I'm just a slave. I can't help you.

RAMONA     Yes you can.

GLORIA     I *won't* help you.

RAMONA     Help me. Help yourself.

      [GLORIA *blows air through her lips. Eyes the ceiling*]

GLORIA     Those are the exact words that you used to get me to break into the boss's safe. That *helped* me to six months in the cellar.

RAMONA     But of course you used those six months wisely. Didn't you.

GLORIA But of course. Hardly a day went by that I didn't use to make myself a better person. Look at me. I'm almost a fucking saint.

RAMONA This may surprise you. But that is not an unusual thing for a saint to be.

[**RAMONA** *stands. Walks to* **GLORIA**. *Taking the brush with her*]

RAMONA I would have expected a conscientious Catholic school girl like yourself to have done more reading between the lines. Take Saint Benedict for example.

[**GLORIA** *just stares at her*]

RAMONA Here. [*Offers her the brush*] Your hair is a mess.

GLORIA I know. I meant to comb it in January but they took away my fork. [*She gets up*] Ah leave me alone. I'm tired. And my bones are making funny scratching noises. I think I've got scurvy or something.

[*She starts slowly toward the door*]

RAMONA This time it's different. I have a plan.

GLORIA Sure. [*opens door*] Hey listen, where's my sister. She just woke me up then disappeared.

RAMONA She's down in the street retrieving something for me.

[*Pause*]

GLORIA How is she anyway.

RAMONA Fine.

GLORIA I guess she was pretty lonely without me.

RAMONA Sit down and wait a minute. She'll be back soon.

[*Long pause.* **GLORIA** *finally nods. Closes door. Sits.* **RAMONA** *is smiling pleasantly.* **GLORIA** *is trying to avoid her eyes*]

GLORIA How's business been?

RAMONA What business?

[**GLORIA** *smiles to herself. Shakes her head.* **LESLIE** *rushes in*]

LESLIE Got it.

[**RAMONA** *takes the envelope*]

RAMONA You took a long time. Did you have any trouble.

LESLIE No. I was looking at the corpse.

GLORIA Looking at what?

LESLIE Hi Gloria. Have a nice sleep?

GLORIA Looking at what?

LESLIE The corpse. I've never seen one before.

GLORIA    What are you making her do.

     [RAMONA *is reading the contents of the envelope*]

RAMONA    Shush. I'm busy.

LESLIE    Oh look. I've got some blood on my stockings. That's awful. I've got to wash them before it sinks in. [*to* RAMONA] What's good for getting out blood.

RAMONA    Busy.

     [LESLIE *starts out*]

GLORIA    Wait. What's that thing over your hand.

LESLIE    I had an accident.

GLORIA    Let me see.

LESLIE    Later.

RAMONA    This is written in German.

GLORIA    [*standing*] Whatya mean later. Let me see your hand, Leslie.

LESLIE    I've got to wash my stockings. They're the only stockings I've got.

RAMONA    Show her.

LESLIE    But.

RAMONA    Show her.

     [LESLIE *shrugs. Pulls off the muffler. She has no hand. She has a golden hook*]

GLORIA    Oh for Christ's sake. [*sits*] What's that?

LESLIE    A hook. A golden hook.

GLORIA    Oh Jesus.

     [RAMONA *hands* LESLIE *the paper*]

RAMONA    You'll have to take this to Wolfy. Do you remember him? He has a little shack down by the squid concession. He'll translate it for us.

LESLIE    Okay. But after I wash my stockings.

RAMONA    Now dear.

LESLIE    [*stomps her foot — upset*] But you don't understand, I hate having dirty —

RAMONA    Now.

     [LESLIE *turns angrily toward the door. Pulls it open.* GLORIA *stands suddenly*]

GLORIA    What happened to her fucking hand!?

LESLIE    [*angrily over her shoulder*] I told you. I had an accident. No one ever listens to me.

[**LESLIE** *leaves. Slams door.* **GLORIA** *is stunned. Sits down*]

**RAMONA**  I'm afraid I'm more or less responsible for the loss of your sister's hand. I'm sorry. [*No response*] Didn't you hear me? I said it was my fault.

[**GLORIA** *is staring, expressionless, ahead*]

**GLORIA**  Was it? [*Pause. Calmly*] That hook is the most obscene thing I have ever —

**RAMONA**  Yes. Yes. But I plan to make it up to her very soon.

**GLORIA**  That's good.

**RAMONA**  I plan to make it up to both of you.

[**GLORIA** *nods.* **RAMONA** *goes to window. Turns back. Looks at* **GLORIA** *for a moment. Turns. Looks out of window. Gloria is still staring ahead*]

**GLORIA**  Where did she get that hook. Did you —

**RAMONA**  No. The bald-headed man gave it to her.

**GLORIA**  Why does it look like that. Why is it so big. Why is it so … shiny.

**RAMONA**  He picked it out especially for her. And he makes her polish it.

**GLORIA**  [*to herself*] He makes her polish it.

[**GLORIA** *is nodding slowly.* **RAMONA** *looks at her over her shoulder*]

[*Blackout*]

# Scene 3

COOK *and* RAMONA. COOK *is opening the window to air the room.* RAMONA *is slowly getting out of bed.*

COOK    A man was beaten to death down there in the street last night.

RAMONA    What happened then.

COOK    I don't understand what you mean. A man was beaten to death.

RAMONA    Was he the same one.

COOK    You're not listening. Listen —

RAMONA    You listen. I'm asking you if he was the same one who was beaten to death last week.

COOK    This opium. Does it —

RAMONA    Opium? What does it have to do with my question. [*a slight stagger. But she is mobile in search of a cigarette*] A man gets beaten to death below my window [*cigarette found and lit*] And I have the right to know who he was.

COOK    I cannot at this time release that information.

RAMONA    But I have reason to believe that it's the same man who has been getting beaten to death below my window for almost a year now. [*in search of brandy decanter*] I must know what happened next. One of two things. A tall bulky man was seen fleeing toward the docks. No one gave chase. Or. A blood-stained club was found on my doorstep and the inspector of police came calling. [*decanter found*] Who are you? [*glass found*]

COOK    Name is Cook. I am with the police.
   [*Brandy poured. Sipped*]

RAMONA    Ah.

COOK    This opium, madame. I must —

RAMONA    Unusually fine. I drift off. Regress. Black out. Fade out. Fade in. All sorts of diversions, you see. And yet I still seem to be ahead of you. The dead man's name was Sebastian. He was a diplomat.

COOK    Perhaps. Do you live here alone.

RAMONA    Yes.

[*Blackout*]

# Scene 4

*Leisure. Ramona is going through a large trunk. Choosing clothes which she places in an open suitcase on the floor.*
*Gloria is sprawled on the couch. Writing in a leather-covered notebook.*
*Leslie is sitting cross-legged on the bed. Reading. And scratching her leg very gently with her hook.*
*A knock at the door.*
*Ignored.*
*A more urgent knock at the door.*
*Ignored.*
*A frantic pounding at the door, followed by a scratching at the door.*

RAMONA  Who is it.

FRIEDRICH  Your Freddy.

RAMONA  Yes, Friedrich. What do you want.

FRIEDRICH  I have a surprise. A terrific surprise.

RAMONA  That's good, Friedrich.

FRIEDRICH  Are you ready?
[*The door swings open.* FRIEDRICH *comes in*]

FRIEDRICH  I have legs! [*he does*]

FRIEDRICH  He gave me legs.
[*He takes two stiff awkward steps. Falls*]

FRIEDRICH  [*grabbing* RAMONA's *skirts*] God bless him, momma. He gave me legs.

RAMONA  Yes. But at what price? [GLORIA *has been shaking her head since* FRIEDRICH *entered*]

GLORIA  Isn't this some kind of miracle or something.
[RAMONA *gets upset*]

RAMONA  He's lying on the floor! If it was a miracle, would he be lying on the floor?!

[*Blackout*]

# Scene 5

*More leisure. Same beginning as in Scene 4, only now*
**FRIEDRICH** *is sitting behind the piano and* **LESLIE** *is reading aloud to him.*

| | |
|---|---|
| **LESLIE** | 'Chapter Two. The Toilet of Venus.' |
| **FRIEDRICH** | No. Skip to Chapter Seven. |
| **LESLIE** | 'Chapter Seven. How Tannhauser Awakened and Took His Morning Ablutions in the Venusberg.' |
| **FRIEDRICH** | No. Never mind. |
| | [**LESLIE** *glares at him. Slams the book closed*] |
| **LESLIE** | What's the matter. Don't you like the way I read to you anymore. |
| **FRIEDRICH** | I want to go for a walk. |
| **LESLIE** | Walking. Walking. That's all you ever think about these days. Walking. |
| | [**RAMONA** *is still going about her business*] |
| **RAMONA** | Yes. Strange, isn't it? And he never plays the piano anymore either. |
| | [**LESLIE** *is staring at* **FRIEDRICH**. *He stands. Takes a couple of difficult steps.* **LESLIE**'s *expression softens*] |
| **LESLIE** | Freddy? |
| **FRIEDRICH** | What? |
| **LESLIE** | I'm sorry. It's just that I liked reading to you. And I liked the way you used to listen. |
| **FRIEDRICH** | I understand. |
| **LESLIE** | Be careful outside. |
| **FRIEDRICH** | [*as he stiffly makes it toward the door*] I get better every day. Yesterday I only fell twenty times. Each time a great thrill came over me. |
| **RAMONA** | Understandable of course. But, the fact remains, that you never play the piano anymore. |
| | [*She finally looks at him. Pause*] |
| **FRIEDRICH** | I will play again, mother. But first I want to learn how to walk. |
| | [*He leaves*] |
| **RAMONA** | He hates me, doesn't he. |
| **LESLIE** | No. |

GLORIA   Yes.

LESLIE   Gloria.

RAMONA   She's right. He hates me. And for some reason the more I feel him hating me the more I feel like giving him reason to hate me more. [*Pause*] But perhaps that's just a normal reaction.

LESLIE   [*a bit confused*] Yes.

GLORIA   No. [*To* RAMONA] Not normal.

RAMONA   Well what's normal these days. The world is at war. People are starving. Behaviour is not what it once was.

GLORIA   You have a real problem. The war will be over. People will be fed. And you will still have a real problem.

    [RAMONA *appears to think this over. Then smiles. Continues with her packing*]

RAMONA   Oh I don't know. I think it might all work out for me in the end. Anyway, it was a mistake to bring it up. Whether he hates me or not. Whether my reaction to him hating me is normal or not. Certain things whould be left unsaid. Especially personal things. They always show weakness. [*She is closely examining a particularly striking dress*] Unless of course there is something to be gained by having certain people react to your weakness. For example, if someone were to attack your weakness then that person would have to drop his or her defences and you would be able to see his or her own weakness. Open bare. Like a wound. Vulnerable. I mean when one attacks one *always* drops one's defences. I think I'll wear this dress on the first day of our freedom. It's totally without remorse. What do you think, Gloria.

    [GLORIA *looks at* RAMONA. *Then goes back to work in her notebook*]

RAMONA   Good. I'll try it on now just to make sure it fits.

    [*She goes behind the dressing partition*]

RAMONA   I've never worn it you know. I bought it on impulse in Lisbon. Just after I buried my husband. But I could never bring myself to wear it until now. [*giggles*] I used to be so weak.

    [GLORIA *looks up. Looks down. Continues writing.* LESLIE *looks at partition. Looks at* GLORIA. *Looks around the room for something to occupy her. Brushes off her skirt. Straightens her collar. Pulls at the cuffs of her blouse. Finally stands. Goes slowly to window. Leans agains the wall. Peeling wallpaper casually with her hook. Looking down into the street*]

LESLIE   They're beating someone up down in the street.

RAMONA   Tell us about it.

LESLIE   They've got him on his knees. And they're kicking him.

RAMONA   Beginning with the weather.

[GLORIA *slams her notebook closed.* LESLIE *looks at* GLORIA. *Then looks out the window again*]

LESLIE   There are clouds in the sky.

RAMONA   What do the clouds look like.

LESLIE   There goes Freddy. Slowly across the street. Slowly. Left foot. Right foot. Left. Oh. He fell. He's up now. He fell again. Up again. Down again. Staying down this time. Crawling. He's crawling. On to the pier. Out to the edge. Into a, what is that? A mist. A fog or something. Crawling into a fog. Disappearing. And there goes Mr. Sebastian. He's followed Freddy into the fog.

RAMONA   The clouds, Leslie.

LESLIE   There are deep grey clouds in the sky. [*Pause*] Low in the sky. And you can't see the sun anywhere. There's no wind except out in the water where there's just a bit. Two sampans are sitting out there and their sails are moving in and out very slowly. In and out. Oh. A large flash of light. Some smoke. One of the sampans is falling apart. Very quickly. It's just sort of crumbling into the water. One sampan on the water with its sail moving in and out slowly. And a bunch of floating wood. And down the street by the pier past the pier where Freddy disappeared in the fog, an old man. I think he's old, lying on the ground covered with newspapers an beside him and old lady doing something. She's ... she's cleaning a rifle. [*Turns around*] Why would she be cleaning a rifle. [*no response. Shrugs. Turns back*] Down in the street below our window they're beating someone up really bad. They've got him on his knees and one of them is holding him by the hair and the other one is kicking him in the stomach and punching him in the face. Now they've put him face down on the ground with his arms behind his back. And one of them has his foot between his legs and now, now they're —

GLORIA   Who's they?

LESLIE  Mister Sebastian's men.

GLORIA  Is the boss down there too?

LESLIE  No. Yes. Yes I think. Yes. Here's Mr. Sebastian now. Coming out of that fog on the pier with a young man.

GLORIA  Freddy?

LESLIE  Yes. No. No, it's not Freddy. It's a young man in a uniform. And he has an airplane pilot's goggles on his head. Mr. Sebastian has his arm around him. They're walking this way. And talking and smiling ... and waving.

> [RAMONA *steps out from behind the dressing partition. She is wearing her silk bathrobe*]

RAMONA  Waving at whom, dear?

LESLIE  Me.

RAMONA  Then wave back. We don't want him to become suspicious.

> [LESLIE *waves*]

GLORIA  Suspicious of what?

RAMONA  Our plans.

GLORIA  What plans.

RAMONA  [*to* LESLIE] Are you smiling.

LESLIE  Should I.

RAMONA  Just a bit.

> [LESLIE *smiles*]

LESLIE  Mr. Sebastian is bringing the young man across the street. I'm smiling. They're right below the window. I'm still smiling. But I don't know if I should be smiling at Mr. Sebastian or the young man. Oh. Never mind. They're coming inside.

> [RAMONA *hurriedly hides the suitcase under the bed.* GLORIA *is looking for a place to hide her notebook*]

RAMONA  When exactly did Wolfy say he would be bringing us the translation.

LESLIE  Yesterday.

RAMONA  Yesterday? Why haven't you mentioned it.

LESLIE  I forgot. I guess I didn't think it was important.

RAMONA  The man who owned the original German document boasted of its worth to me not five minutes before he was killed. With that document we have the means for escape. Didn't I tell you that?

LESLIE  No.

GLORIA  No.

RAMONA     A little oversight. My apologies. Where is it?
         [LESLIE *takes it out of her pocket. Hands it to* RAMONA.
         GLORIA *is frantic*]

GLORIA     Where can I hide this.

RAMONA     Why hide it at all. It's just your diary, isn't it.

GLORIA     No. It's not my diary. Where can I hide it. If the boss finds it, he'll
         destroy it out of spite.

RAMONA     Give it here. [GLORIA *just stares at her*] All right, then give it to
         Leslie. [GLORIA *hands it to* LESLIE]

RAMONA     If they ask tell them it's a secret. Then giggle like an idiot.

LESLIE     All right.

RAMONA     Remember. None of us should look too hopeful. The bald-
         headed man can detect hopefulness very quickly. Everyone
         relax. Look indifferent. Breathe slowly.
         [GLORIA *suddenly grabs the notebook from* LESLIE. *Looks at*
         RAMONA. *Sits*]

LESLIE     [*looking out the window*] I think he's dead. They've stopped
         kicking him. [*turns toward the others*] The man in the street.
         [*Lights start to fade. Pause*]

LESLIE     Oh. Look. The cannibals.

[*Blackout*]
[*A knock at the door*]

# Scene 6

COOK *and* RAMONA

COOK    I must ask you some questions about the deceased.

RAMONA    He was a good enough man. Except that he floundered in times of crises. And sometimes used people.

COOK    How old was he.

RAMONA    I don't know exactly. Fifty.

COOK    He was your employer?

RAMONA    What do you mean?

        *[They stare at each other]*

COOK    Well what was your relationship with him.

RAMONA    I knew him. He lived here. And I knew him.

COOK    Did the two of you live here alone.

RAMONA    We almost always had guests in the house.

COOK    The two sisters. From that private Catholic school.

RAMONA    For a while.

COOK    The young aviator.

RAMONA    Briefly.

COOK    Where are they now.

RAMONA    Why are you asking me.

COOK    They're missing.

RAMONA    Missing from where.

COOK    Just missing.

RAMONA    How unfortunate.

        *[Pause]*

COOK    Back to the deceased. Could you describe your relationship with him in more detail.

RAMONA    No.

COOK    Did you hate him.

RAMONA    Of course not. He gave my son legs.

COOK    I beg your pardon.

RAMONA    I have a son. Friedrich. He looks like his father. His father was murdered many years ago.

COOK    I know.

RAMONA    Yes I suppose you do know. Being from the police, I mean. Listen, did you ever find out who murdered him.

COOK    No.

RAMONA    Too bad.

COOK    Some day, perhaps.

RAMONA    That would be nice. [*Pause*] My son. Friedrich. He lost his legs in an accident when he was two years old. Accident was my fault, I'm afraid.

COOK    And Mr. Sebastian gave him new legs?

RAMONA    Yes. [*Smiles*]

COOK    Is that some kind of joke.

    [**RAMONA** *gets upset*]

RAMONA    I was once a bride of Christ! What kind of disgusting perversion do you think I have in my mind to be joking about my sons legs!?

    [**RAMONA** *is staring hard at* **COOK**. *He loosens his collar a bit*]

        [*Fade out*]

# Scene 7

*Lights up.* RAMONA *and* COOK.
COOK *is powdering* RAMONA's *neck.*

RAMONA    Very sweet of you to do this.

COOK    Tell me. Where is your son.

RAMONA    I don't know. He went away to learn how to walk. He'll come back someday though. His piano is here. And his music.

COOK    He was a composer?

RAMONA    Dissonant and bewildering. His music was unique but it took some getting used to. Nevertheless he could have been a great artist. Getting those legs was the worst thing that could ever have happened to him. [*lights a cigarette*] I am sick to death of your innuendo! Just say what you mean, sir.

COOK    I beg your pardon.

RAMONA    Yes. He was a composer. He left home because I ignored him. No. He left home because he ignored me. Truth is this. I only kept him around because he reminded me of his father. No, I —

COOK    I understand.

RAMONA    Actually he was a bit of a fop. I think he crawled all the way to London to meet his decadent heroes. [*She begins a lengthy search of the room*] Many things have happened since my fall from innocence. I wasn't made for the convent. I used it to get away from home. Miguel was too intricate a man to be a priest. A big man. The Orient does strange things to your body. Your mind is safe if you put it somewhere else but your body takes to bizarre cravings and subtle forces make it move in many different ways. Be sure I'm the first one informed if and when you find Miguel's murderer.

COOK    After all these years —

RAMONA    Yes, yes, difficult I know —

COOK    Then the fact that you took the body away so quickly without letting the authorities examine —

RAMONA    Yes, yes. I don't know why I did that. Probably hysterical. Always meant to apologize to the authorities. Could never find them. They hide so well here, don't you think.

COOK    I couldn't say. [*Long pause. While she intensifies her search*]

RAMONA   Do you think I'm a manipulating person.

COOK   I don't know.

RAMONA   No more so than others. Everyone manipulates in one situation or another. Sometime in their lives.

COOK   That's true.

RAMONA   Is it? [*Nods*] Yes. Well, listen you might be interested in knowing that Mr. Sebastian, the dead man, used to powder my neck like you were doing. Not nearly so well, though.

[*She has found it. A small white envelope. She opens it. Smells*]

RAMONA   Would you care for some mescaline?

[*Cook reaches into his pocket. Produces a larger white envelope. Holds it up. Smiles*]

[*Blackout*]

# Scene 8

GLORIA *and* RAMONA *are sitting on the floor in a corner. A large*
*map spread out in front of them. In whispers they are referring to*
*'the document' occasionally making marks or drawing lines on*
*the map. They are passing a pipe back and forth.*
*Every once in a while one of them will giggle or groan or some-*
*thing.* LESLIE *sits on the floor in the middle of the room, looking*
*up at a man, enthralled. It is* FRIEDRICH, *who comes to us now as*
MITCH *the young aviator. In German (W.W.I) pilot's uniform.*
*Tunic undone. Bare-chested. Sweating. Highly active. Apparently*
*self-confident. He is, in effect, a new man. And therefore not*
*recognizable to the ladies. He speaks with a slight German ac-*
*cent.*

MITCH   It was smash-up time on the Western front. Buzz-bombers cutting through the night. A high-pitched screaming over your
head. Splinters ripping through the air. Across the field. And into
the barracks. Wheezing. Then bursting into flames. Then falling
apart in smoke. A hundred of our boys burning in their sleep but
Ralphe and I were at the canteen too drunk to make it home and
now we're shouting at each other as we run into the field. From
trench to trench. Looking for our planes. Trying to get our leather
on. Rolling along the ground. Crawling across the field. And
here's one jack in the box flying so low he's dodging his own
bombs trying to put his bullets in your mouth. I turn my head just
in time to see him cut Ralphe's body into a thousand little pieces.
But I've seen my plane so I keep twisting and running like hell.
Hurdling these huge craters. Gagging in the smoke. And running
till I'm at her wing, then quick like a rabbit into her cockpit
turning her over, spinning her around down the runway into the
pitch black praying so hard I think I had my eyes closed. And
then up and farther up until I'm in amongst them. Giving them a
bit of their own and a bit more to spare. Staying up there. Staying
for hours. Until the sun came up and they'd all fart-assed it
home. Leaving me all alone up in the sky and nothing but wre-
ckage on the ground.

    [*He sits down beside* LESLIE. *But he is still twitching a bit*]

LESLIE    How often did things like that happen.

MITCH    Twice a week.

LESLIE    Isn't that something.

MITCH    That's why sometimes I have trouble relaxing [*Looks at his shaking hand*] After living like that its very hard to come down.
> [**LESLIE** *puts her one hand around his shaking hand. Rests her hook on top of her hand*]

LESLIE    Isn't that something. Gloria, did you hear what Mitch was saying? [*no response*] Isn't that something though.

MITCH    Yes. I guess so. But mostly I don't like to talk about it. Because it wasn't pleasant.
> [**LESLIE** *is watching her hook bob up and down.* **MITCH** *notices. Takes away his hand. Puts it behind his back*]

LESLIE    Is there anything I can do for you now.

MITCH    Like what.

LESLIE    Anything. I'll do anything for you. I'll do anything for anybody. That's my nature.

MITCH    [*smiles*] That's funny.

LESLIE    No it's not. But I can't help it. That's the way I am.

MITCH    Then you're very special.

LESLIE    I am? How?
> [**MITCH** *just smiles quizzically*]

LESLIE    Tell me. Look at me. And tell me exactly how I'm special.

MITCH    Well. Well you're ... clean. You're very clean. You're the cleanest person I've ever seen in my life. [*Looking closely*] There's ... not ... a ... spot ... on you ...

LESLIE    Thank you.

MITCH    You're welcome. [*Leans back on his elbows*] They don't like me.

LESLIE    Sure they do.

MITCH    Then why are they ignoring me.

LESLIE    They're busy.

MITCH    Tell the truth. They don't like me. Do they?

LESLIE    Not much. I'm sorry.

MITCH    That's all right. People in general don't.

LESLIE    Why not.

MITCH    I think it's because they see through me.

LESLIE    I see through you. And I like you.

MITCH    You're probably the type who likes everyone.

LESLIE    That's true.
        *[Pause]*
MITCH    Why are you a whore?
        *[RAMONA and GLORIA look up]*
LESLIE    I'm not a whore, Mitch. I'm a slave.
MITCH    Oh.
        *[RAMONA and GLORIA go back to their business. MITCH and LESLIE have gradually become more intimate. MITCH is playing with her hook. Licking it. LESLIE is becoming aroused. GLORIA is watching them out of the corner of her eye]*
MITCH    How did you get to be a slave.
LESLIE    I can't remember. I have a blank spot about it. And everytime I ask Gloria she just says I'm better off not remembering.
MITCH    I'll ask her for you if you want.
LESLIE    No. I wouldn't do that.
MITCH    Why not.
LESLIE    Because she'll slit your throat. She told me she'd just as soon slit your throat as talk to you. I think she means it too. She just hasn't been the same since they let her out of the cellar. She's been acting very crabby. And very very strange.
        *[LESLIE has been almost swooning during preceding speech. Suddenly MITCH takes her hook and shoves it violently between his legs. LESLIE gasps and lunges for his neck. GLORIA stands. RAMONA restrains her. MITCH is staring at GLORIA. He pushes LESLIE away quietly. She is trying to catch her breath. Pause]*
MITCH    Can we go back to your room.
LESLIE    You go ahead. I'll only be a minute.
        *[MITCH gets up. Walks to the door. Watching GLORIA as he leaves. Opens door. Turns to LESLIE]*
MITCH    Do me a favour.
LESLIE    What?
MITCH    Don't take your hook off. I know it's just a gimmick. But I like it.
        *[He leaves. LESLIE looks at her hook for a moment. Tries half-heartedly to take it off. Then stands. Brushes herself off. Straightens her clothes]*

**LESLIE**   I'm going back to my room for a while.

**GLORIA**   Get rid of that asshole, will ya.

**LESLIE**   He's lonely.

**GLORIA**   He's a fraud. If I hear another one of those long boring bullshit stories I'm gonna start screaming and never stop.

**LESLIE**   Why don't you like them. I like them.

**GLORIA**   Well you see little sister. He's not telling the truth. He's telling lies. I don't like lies.

**LESLIE**   Oh come on, you do so like lies, Gloria.

**GLORIA**   What?

**LESLIE**   You like lies.

[**GLORIA** *stands*]

**GLORIA**   What the hell do you mean?

**LESLIE**   Why are you getting upset.

**GLORIA**   What the hell do you mean I like lies!?

[**GLORIA** *suddenly rushes* **LESLIE**. **LESLIE** *is startled. Raises her hook*]

**LESLIE**   Are you going to hit me.

**RAMONA**   You're scaring your sister, Gloria.

[**GLORIA** *sees the hook. Stops. Backs away. Staring at the hook*]

**GLORIA**   I just want to know why she's saying stupid things.

**LESLIE**   She was going to hit me.

**RAMONA**   She's just upset because you're spending so much time with that man.

**LESLIE**   I like him!

**RAMONA**   Of course. But be careful. He's obviously a psychopath.

**LESLIE**   But you say that Mr. Sebastian is a psychopath too.

**RAMONA**   And he is, dear.

**LESLIE**   But you weren't careful, were you.

**RAMONA**   [*standing*] What was that.

**LESLIE**   I said, you weren't careful!

[**RAMONA** *rushes toward* **LESLIE**]

**LESLIE**   [*backing up*] Gloria.

[**GLORIA** *grabs* **RAMONA**. **LESLIE** *is making her way through the door*]

**LESLIE**   Why is everyone getting so upset. I'm just telling the truth. I'm sorry.

[*She slams the door.* RAMONA *frees herself from* GLORIA*'s grasp. Firmly but graciously. They look at each other.* RAMONA *opens the door*]

RAMONA  I'm sorry too, dear.

GLORIA  You see what I mean about her? That boy's been here for three days. And she's been talking stupid like that for three days. I think he has her on narcotics.

[*They look at each other. Giggle. Sober up quickly*]

RAMONA  If he's still here tomorrow I'll kill him.

GLORIA  No. I'll kill him.

RAMONA  If you don't mind?

GLORIA  Why should I mind?

[*Pleasant smiles*]

RAMONA  How exactly will you kill him.

GLORIA  I'm going to eat him. [*Chuckles. Falls on to the bed*]

RAMONA  [*chuckles*] I like that. Oh. That reminds me.

[*She goes to window*]

GLORIA  What are you doing.

RAMONA  Looking for the cannibals. I have a message for them from the Christian God.

GLORIA  That's not funny.

RAMONA  What, the cannibals or the Christian God?

GLORIA  The combination.

RAMONA  I knew a priest once who ate people alive.

GLORIA  So what.

RAMONA  Well I think that's funny.

GLORIA  One priest doesn't represent God anymore than you represent motherhood.

[RAMONA *steps closer. Curiously, looks* GLORIA *over*]

RAMONA  You're still a believer. Very strange.

GLORIA  Even stranger that you are too.

RAMONA  Not true. In fact I never was.

GLORIA  The insanely dedicated bride of Christ. When all the other brides had gone to sleep you were still up waiting for him to come to bed. 'Come wrap your scrawny arms around me. I'm yours forever. I was born to be yours. Even when I leave the church and crawl around in all the world's dirt I'll still be yours. Love me. I'm obsessive.'

[**RAMONA** *smiles. Pats* **GLORIA** *on the head*]

RAMONA  What an ugly little speech.

GLORIA  I know. I think I've become a bit unbalanced.

RAMONA  Are you blaming me?

GLORIA  Yes.

RAMONA  Then who should I blame.

[*She turns away*]

GLORIA  Don't bother blaming anyone. You'll always be deranged. Some people are just born that way. Bad luck. For all of us.

[*Pause.* **RAMONA** *has made her way back to the corner. Is sitting now with her finger on the map*]

RAMONA  From Bombay we take the train to Casablanca. And from Casablanca we —

GLORIA  I read that thing. It doesn't say anything about going to Casablanca. What is all this Casablanca shit.

RAMONA  I know someone there. I met him on the way back from burying Miguel.

GLORIA  You met a lot of people on that trip.

RAMONA  Yes. But I was too weak in the mind to enjoy them. I could enjoy them now I think.

[*They look at each other. Smile. A knock at the door*]

SEBASTIAN  May I come in.

RAMONA  One moment.

GLORIA  Where's the nail file.

RAMONA  On the wash stand.

[**RAMONA** *hides the map and the 'the document' under the mattress. Sits on the bed. Takes off her slippers. Extends one leg.* **GLORIA** *has found the file. She sits on the floor. Working on* **RAMONA**'s *toe nails*]

RAMONA  Look at us. It's just like I was your ... And you were my ...

SEBASTIAN  May I come in!

GLORIA  Let him in.

RAMONA  Yes. You may came in.

[**SEBASTIAN** *comes in. A frail seedy-looking man. Wearing a white suit. Sunglasses. A broad-rimmed black hat. Lots of jewelry*]

SEBASTIAN  Why was I kept waiting.

RAMONA  [*very quietly*] I'm sorry.

| | |
|---|---|
| SEBASTIAN | Speak up. |
| RAMONA | I'm sorry. |
| SEBASTIAN | What are you doing in here, little girl. |
| GLORIA | Filing the lady's toe nails, boss. |
| SEBASTIAN | You seem to be spending a lot of time in here. Why is that. Don't you like your own room anymore. |
| RAMONA | She hasn't been spending that much – |
| SEBASTIAN | I asked *her.* |
| GLORIA | I've never liked my own room, boss. It hasn't got a view. This is the only room with a view. |
| SEBASTIAN | Except for the cellar. Which has the same view as this. Only from a different angle. |
| GLORIA | That's right. [*Smiles*] |
| SEBASTIAN | Then you liked your stay in the cellar? |
| GLORIA | Oh very much. It was very nice. |
| SEBASTIAN | Well perhaps you can visit there again. |
| GLORIA | Okay. Whatever you say. |
| SEBASTIAN | Leave us. |
| GLORIA | Yes, boss. |
| SEBASTIAN | Quickly. |
| GLORIA | Yes, boss. |

[*She leaves. They watch her go. Watch the door close. Wait. Then* **RAMONA** *goes to the wash stand. Pours water from the pitcher in the basin. Begins to give herself a light bath*]

| | |
|---|---|
| SEBASTIAN | The police came by this morning. About that man that was killed in the street. |
| RAMONA | But I thought your men removed the body. |
| SEBASTIAN | They did. But that's not the man I'm referring to. The other one. Your friend. Elliot. The one who was stabbed when he left here. |
| RAMONA | I remember. Did the police ask you many questions. |
| SEBASTIAN | None. They're too discreet. No they were merely bringing me some information which I requested about the deceased. |
| RAMONA | And why should you be so curious about him? |
| SEBASTIAN | He was a client of – |
| RAMONA | Friend. |
| SEBASTIAN | He was a friend of yours. I wanted to find out who killed him. |
| RAMONA | Who killed him? |
| SEBASTIAN | A hired assassin. |

| | |
|---|---|
| **RAMONA** | Hired by whom? |
| **SEBASTIAN** | You. |
| **RAMONA** | You silly man. |
| **SEBASTIAN** | You deny it then. |
| **RAMONA** | Well who must I deny it to. Who is accusing me. |
| **SEBASTIAN** | Do you also deny that you told Leslie that he was a famous archeologist when in fact he was just a salesman for a cosmetics firm. |
| **RAMONA** | How do you know what I told Leslie. |
| **SEBASTIAN** | I overheard her telling the young aviator. |
| **RAMONA** | What else did you overhear. |
| **SEBASTIAN** | Plenty. |
| **RAMONA** | [*over her shoulder*] The truth. |
| **SEBASTIAN** | Nothing. I coughed. And they overheard me overhearing them and began to whisper. |
| **RAMONA** | You spy on the girls a great deal. |
| **SEBASTIAN** | It's the only way I can find out what you're up to. |
| **RAMONA** | Amazing. How much you've changed. How small you've become. Almost like you were intended to be this small all along. And that that very big man you once were was just a distortion of someone's youth. That man wouldn't spy on anyone. He had his mind always on loftier things. Or so it appeared anyway. |
| **SEBASTIAN** | [*whispering*] That man is dead. |
| **RAMONA** | What? |
| **SEBASTIAN** | [*quietly*] That man is dead. |
| **RAMONA** | What? |
| **SEBASTIAN** | That man is dead! |
| **RAMONA** | Figuratively speaking, of course. |
| **SEBASTIAN** | [*whispers*] Of course. [*Corrects himself*] Of course. |
| **RAMONA** | Here. Powder the back of my neck. |
| | [*She hands him the powder and pad. He proceeds to powder her*] |
| **SEBASTIAN** | Nevertheless, I feel I have the right to know what you are planning. |
| **RAMONA** | I tell you, you're just a tiny bit too small to have rights. However, if you stay out of my way your life might be spared. |
| **SEBASTIAN** | But why can't — |

RAMONA [*turns on him*] And the questions must stop! There must be no more questions! You can spy all you want, sneak around and whine till your heart's content. But there must be no more questions. And when the time comes you must do exactly as I say. Then get out of the way. Or I will have you cut apart. Do you understand that.

SEBASTIAN Yes.

RAMONA Good. That's really all you want now isn't it. To be left alive. Isn't it?

SEBASTIAN Yes. Please leave me alive.

[*She turns away*]

RAMONA [*chuckles*] Ah you're such a naughty man. Giving people legs and golden hooks. Some day they'll catch you and lock you up. And quite rightly too. Naughty man playing God. Playing our sweet Jesus Christ. Miracles indeed. Can a lizard make miracles? You must be quite mad.

[*Sebastian is shaking his head slowly*]

RAMONA Powder my neck.

[*Blackout*]
[*Music, Piano. Strange. Aloof*]

# Scene 9

LESLIE *is looking out the window.* GLORIA *is sitting on the*
*couch. Writing in her notebook. Very morose.*
RAMONA *is high. Effusive. Kinetic. Packing again. But with*
*abandon. Laughing a lot.*

RAMONA     Oh yes. He was a very famous archeologist. And he had access to
a spectacular find somewhere in the upper third of the African
Continent. He spent most of his adult life trying to pinpoint the
exact location. Then he became involved somehow in the in-
trigue of this foolish war and lost his life before he was able to
consummate the dream. But somewhere in the upper third of the
African Continent buried behind cave walls the secrets of an
older civilization lie waiting.

LESLIE     There's a little boy wetting his pants down in the gutter. A sailor
and a lady dwarf are exchanging foreign currency. The sailor is
looking down the lady dwarf's blouse. The snow is melting off
the top of the mountain. And five junk boats are setting out to
sea.
           [GLORIA *looks at* LESLIE. *Looks at* RAMONA]

GLORIA     When do we leave.

RAMONA     Imagine what's there. This older civilization waiting. Its beauty
and its disgrace. Glazed vases, gold embedded in cloth, statues,
pots and countless little precious things all finer than the jewels
of kings.

LESLIE     The lady dwarf is selling the little boy to the sailor. He's taking
him away.

RAMONA     Or new found kings finer than the now found kings. And many
more things as well that we can use to give ourselves hope,
dignity and personal freedom. And yet I am not such a fool as to
forget that all bones will eventually lie bare and no distinction
will be made between those who lived without hope and those
who had it. Because when the bones lie bare they do not awaken
and we are all doomed doomed doomed. But in the meantime –

GLORIA     When do we leave.

RAMONA     I didn't know you were in a hurry.

GLORIA     My sister's going crazy and I have to get her out of here.

LESLIE    That's not nice, Gloria. Besides, I've decided I'm not leaving. I'm in love.

GLORIA    With that little maniac?

LESLIE    Yes. My darling little maniac.

GLORIA    You're leaving with me.

RAMONA    With us.

LESLIE    Only if he comes too.

[GLORIA *is wiping off the blade of a knife*]

RAMONA    What are you doing with that knife.

GLORIA    When are we leaving.

RAMONA    When we're fully prepared.

GLORIA    How long will that take.

RAMONA    Not too long. The knife?

GLORIA    I figure that no matter how you plan it we'll have to get past at least one of them. I mean there's always one of them watching. The boss or one of his men. Preferably the boss. And I'm going to be there. With this. Cutting. Cutting very deep.

LESLIE    No one watches me. I come and go as I want.

GLORIA    That's because they think you're simple-minded.

LESLIE    That's not nice. They have no right to think that about me. I'm not at all simple-minded. I'm just pleasant.

GLORIA    The same thing.

LESLIE    It is not.

[GLORIA *stands. Goes to window*]

GLORIA    Oh yeah? Where's the mountain.

LESLIE    What?

GLORIA    Where the snow's melting. The mountain. The one you were just talking about.

LESLIE    I don't understand —

[GLORIA *grabs* LESLIE. *Turns her around toward* RAMONA]

GLORIA    Look at this. Look at her eyes. Who's doing this to her.

LESLIE    You're wrinkling my dress.

GLORIA    Who's giving you drugs. Mitch? The boss? Who?

LESLIE    I don't take drugs.

GLORIA    [*shaking her*] You're lying.

LESLIE    I am not. You're ripping my dress.

[LESLIE *pushes* GLORIA *away with her hook.* GLORIA *stares at her. Then turns to* RAMONA]

GLORIA   I'm going to my room to sleep. Don't wake me until all this stops. Until you stop singing about African kings and bare bones. Until she stops babbling about what's outside that window. Until it's time to leave. When it's time to leave just wake me and point me in the direction of whoever it is who's going to be in my way.

[GLORIA *leaves.* RAMONA *goes over and picks up* GLORIA's *notebook*]

LESLIE   She wants to kill someone. Is that right?

RAMONA   Yes.

LESLIE   I don't understand her.

RAMONA   How can you. You're so young.

LESLIE   I used to. She was my sister and I understood that. We talked. Then something happened. Is that right.

RAMONA   I don't know.

LESLIE   Yes. Something happened. Can't remember what exactly. Sometimes I want to ask her things still. But she's become strange. Writing in her book. I don't know what. Do you?

RAMONA   I think so.

LESLIE   What?

RAMONA   You're too young.

LESLIE   I mean to ask her myself. Then I look out the window, see all those things out there. Forget. I don't understand her. Is she a mean person.

RAMONA   Yes. She's a very mean person.

LESLIE   Then we should try to help her.

RAMONA   Don't you worry about it, dear. You just do what you're doing. I'll help her.

LESLIE   Okay. You help her. I'll help Mitch.

RAMONA   Oh yes. Mitch. He needs help, does he?

LESLIE   Lots.

RAMONA   You know dear. There are some men who come into your life who are not what they seem. Weak men in disguises. Men who you've known before and treated like a child or a friend. Building themselves up in their disguises so you'll treat them like a lover now. These men keep coming back into your life all the time. But you have to remember you knew them before. When they were children. Because beneath their disguises they're still what they were. They haven't changed.

LESLIE  I don't understand that.

RAMONA  No. How could you. Never mind. Just out of curiosity, who do you love more, your sister or me?

LESLIE  Mitch.

RAMONA  Oh. Does he love you.

LESLIE  I don't know.

  [*Pause*]

RAMONA  Would you like him to.

LESLIE  That would be nice.

RAMONA  Would you like him to come with us.

LESLIE  Extra nice.

RAMONA  Consider it done. Go send him into me.

LESLIE  But how —

RAMONA  Now.

  [LESLIE *runs out.* RAMONA *puts a record on the phonograph. Winds it up. Sits down on the couch. Slightly dazed. Staring off. The music is gentle. Sensual. After a moment or two, a knock at the door.* RAMONA *turns her head slowly. Stares at the door for a while before answering*]

RAMONA  Come in.

  [MITCH *comes in. Wearing a bathrobe. Rubbing his eyes.* RAMONA *gets up. Goes to him. Undoes the belt in one swift motion. Takes off his bathrobe. Immediately turns away.* MITCH *has scars that go completely around both his legs, and has bandages around his entire mid-section*]

RAMONA  Lie on the bed. Face down.

  [MITCH *does so.* RAMONA *gets some oil from her dressing table. Then goes and sits on the side of the bed. Begins to give* MITCH *a massage. Slow gentle massage. Slow gentle voice*]

RAMONA  Did you sleep well.

MITCH  No. I never sleep well.

RAMONA  Why is that?

MITCH  I don't know. Maybe I'm disturbed.

RAMONA  Possibly. Your muscles are very tense. Relax.

MITCH  All right.

  [*Pause*]

RAMONA  How would you like to go on an adventure.

MITCH        I've just come back from one. I need a rest from adventure. I'm
             having bad dreams.

RAMONA       Tell me about them.

MITCH        No.

RAMONA       I know your problem. You're afraid that you're all alone. And the
             truth is sad. You are. But I can offer you company and affection.

MITCH        I've heard it all before, lady.

RAMONA       Oh really. What a tough worldly young man you are.

MITCH        Yeah.

RAMONA       That's too bad. Because our Leslie is growing very fond of you.
             And she could be just what you need. If you weren't so ... tough.

MITCH        Is she going with you.

RAMONA       Yes.

MITCH        She told me she wasn't.

RAMONA       She lied.

MITCH        That's too bad. I was just getting comfortable.

RAMONA       You could come too.

MITCH        Is it far?

RAMONA       Not so far.

MITCH        How far?

RAMONA       North Africa.

MITCH        Oh. I've got bad memories of North Africa. I killed an entire
             company of men there.

RAMONA       Your own?

MITCH        Of course not. The enemy.

RAMONA       Then they shouldn't be too hard to forget.

MITCH        What do you know. Have you ever killed a man with your bare
             hands.

RAMONA       Yes.

                  [MITCH *looks up at her*]

RAMONA       There's more at stake than you realize.

MITCH        Maybe.

RAMONA       Have you always been a soldier.

MITCH        I don't know. I have a blank spot. A big one. Probably yes.
             Probably my blank spot is from shell shock. I mean look at me I
             was obviously a born soldier.

RAMONA       Yes. [*She touches one of his scars*] What awful scars.

MITCH        [*groans*] Be careful. They're not quite healed.

[*The massage becomes more sexual. Slightly more daring.*
*MITCH reacts slowly at first. Then begins to writhe. The wri-*
*thing becomes gradually more active*]

RAMONA  Give up your foolish wars. I see you lying in a jungle clearing. Grey- haired and paunchy. Cut open at the throat by some rebel's machete. The death of a professional soldier. No one to notify. No one to mourn. Dead and rotting and so what.

MITCH  Yeah. I can see that. That makes sense.

RAMONA  Think about it.

MITCH  I am.

RAMONA  How much money do you have.

MITCH  A thousand.

RAMONA  Not really enough. Tonight you'll break into the bald-headed man's office. Behind the painting of St. Benedict's temptation you'll find a wall safe. The combination is 1 - 12 - 43. Three to the left, then right, then left. 1 - 12 -

MITCH  1 - 12

RAMONA  43. Wait for my signal. I'll create a diversion.

MITCH  What is the purpose of this adventure.

RAMONA  It varies.

MITCH  It's a terrible thought, isn't it. Dying in middle age of a cut throat and nobody to care.

RAMONA  1 - 12 - 43.

MITCH  Three to the left.

RAMONA  Then right. Then left.

MITCH  [*slowly breathing deeply*] Left. Right. Left. Right. Left. -

RAMONA  Now turn over.

[*He looks up at her. She begins to unbutton her bathrobe. He begins to turn over.*

[*Blackout*]

# Scene 10

RAMONA *is sitting on the bed. Staring off. Holding* MITCH's
*bathrobe. He has gone.*
GLORIA *bursts through the door. Hyper. Perspiring.*

GLORIA     Somebody took my notebook. Was it you. [*no response*] Was it you?

RAMONA     Why me —

GLORIA     Don't know. Don't — I'm going to search your room.

RAMONA     Go ahead.

           [GLORIA *begins to search. No concentration. Searching some places two or three times. Leaving others untouched*]

RAMONA     It must be important to you.

GLORIA     Yes it is. Now where is it.

           [*But* RAMONA *has put on a cape and is walking out the door*]

GLORIA     I asked you a question you cocky bitch.

RAMONA     You've had a terrible problem since you were a little girl. You're an addict. You've used that notebook to avoid facing reality. You're addicted to it, Gloria. And that's why we have to get you away from here. To cure you. Now try to calm yourself. Use cold water. [*She leaves*]

GLORIA     Addict? What's she mean 'addict'! I just want my notebook. That's all. What's she mean. [*Runs to window. Shouts out*] I asked you a question! Why are you pretending I didn't.

           [*The door opens.* SEBASTIAN *is standing there.* GLORIA *turns around suddenly*]

GLORIA     No one's following her. I mean she's just walking down the street and no one's following her.

SEBASTIAN     I know.

GLORIA     Well why. She says we can't do that. We're trapped here.

SEBASTIAN     Why don't I have any rights.

GLORIA     You did this to me! You and her!

SEBASTIAN     Why does she call me the bald-headed man.

GLORIA     She told us that you had become deranged. That you were dangerous and had to be obeyed.

SEBASTIAN     But why does she always call me the bald-headed man.

GLORIA     [*sits down*] That you wanted to keep us locked up. With no money and no dignity and charge people to punish us with indecent acts so that you could get filthy rich and perform miracles like giving people food and shelter and legs and golden hooks. That you had become evil and ugly and very very small and that that was why we were the way we were with so much trouble in the mind and so many things we couldn't remember, because a long time ago you used to be so different, you used to be — [*Tries to stand*] used to be — [*Falls back*]

SEBASTIAN   Why does she call me the bald-headed man. Why don't I have any rights. Why does she always keep me waiting. Why do I ask so many questions. Used to be what? Used to be what.
   [*He leaves.* GLORIA *watches him go*]

GLORIA   What are they doing?
   [*She stands. Goes to window*]

GLORIA   Look at that stupid beggar down there. And there's another one. Every time I look out this window all I see is slime. Where's the mountain. I can't see no fucking mountain.
   [GLORIA *is staring off. Lights start to fade.* GLORIA *turns away from the window. Suddenly turns back*]

[*Blackout*]

# Scene 11

COOK *and* RAMONA. RAMONA *under the street lamp.* COOK *leaning out the window.*

RAMONA   Leave me alone, mister policeman. I'm not hurting anybody.

COOK   I was just wondering if you'd care to rejoin me.

RAMONA   It's too muggy in there. And the concierge hasn't changed the linen in a month. Dust on all the ledges. Smell of piss in the little boy's room. The place is suffering from indifferent management. No. Thank you anyway. I'll just stay down here until my heart stops palpitating. I think I almost overdosed.

COOK   I have some more questions to ask you.

RAMONA   Concerning the deceased? Or the missing?

COOK   Both.

RAMONA   Oh go away and come back some Tuesday afternoon. What do you want — a confession? All right. I did it.

COOK   Try to be exact. Did what?

RAMONA   No I did not. I just didn't. And that's all there is to it.

COOK   Why don't you come inside.

RAMONA   Guilt will only stretch so far, you know. Clean out the psyche then get rid of it. If you don't you get pathetic. I never intended to become pathetic. [*Turns toward him*] Your suspicions are not necessarily on course, sir.

COOK   I've never said that I —

RAMONA   Never mind that. I'll tell you the truth if you're interested.

        [*Pause*]

COOK   Go ahead.

RAMONA   Oh the mind sometimes snaps. You mismanage a situation. Invite the wrong people. Have the wrong children with the wrong father. So you wait until you think they're all old enough, strong enough, then you invite them into play. Think it's time to open up your head to them. Expose them to the disease. Thinking it will give them immunity. Or maybe you don't think at all. Mind snaps. Thinking stops. Makes sense? So you don't think. Just need. Use what's around. Whoever. The girls were around you see. My son was going away. Actually he'd gone away long before. And he'd make it clear that he wasn't coming back. It took him twenty-seven years to make it all the way to my bedroom door. The fact that he was given those idiotic legs is neither here nor there. I just figure someone was trying to rub it in. Thinking back though I guess the legs were supposed to give him dignity. Foolish really. You don't need dignity for leaving. You need it for staying. Forget the legs. They don't mean anything. His father once had legs. Muscular legs. Gentle muscles. You could feel them harden but you could never see them. Punishment! That's what I'm talking about. Punishment for all concerned. See but don't touch. Feel but never see. Find something. Lose something. Punish others. Punish yourself. For crimes pre-meditated. For crimes just committed. [*Pause*] Unreasonable. Self-inflicted. Punishment.

    [*Long pause*]

**COOK**    Oh, really.

**RAMONA**    Punishment. And love. It came to me late one night after a particularly degrading episode with a client from somewhere in the American mid-west. He wanted me to urinate on him and cut into his nipples with my finger nails. I got rid of him. But things like that have a way of putting your mind into a nervous gallop. It occurred to me that I had to arrange for Leslie to lose her hand. Some people just aren't bothered by a handicap. Leslie was one of those. She would be all right. Just sever the hand and make sure she got immediate medical attention. I would in fact save her life. She'd be grateful. Never leave. Simple. And when Gloria found out − amazing Gloria, who was still somehow religious in her own bizarre way − I would have her too. Hanging there suspended by her hatred. And unable to let it out. You see Gloria was an addict. No I was an addict. No Gloria − No what's it matter. One of us was and it might as well have been all of us − even Leslie. Gloria, Leslie. I wanted them both to stay. Never leave. Like any woman any mother who's son was going away who'd actually gone away. I would have them both. Love. Do you see what love can do? What a powerful and inventive thing it is?

    [*Blackout*]
    [**COOK** *chuckles in the darkness*]

# Scene 12

*Late evening.* **GLORIA** *is waiting at the door. Shivering. Arms wrapped around body.*
*Footsteps up the stairs.*
**GLORIA** *makes herself ready.*
**RAMONA** *opens the door. Comes in.*

RAMONA     Ah good. I've just been making last minute plans. We leave tonight.
       [**GLORIA** *approaches her slowly*]

GLORIA     Don't. Fuck. With me. Lady.
       [**RAMONA** *casually turns away. Takes off her cape*]

GLORIA     Did you hear me?

RAMONA     I did. [*Turns toward her*] But I don't know what you mean.

GLORIA     Don't do that. That twinkle in your eye thing. I'm not my little sister. No little baby doll.

RAMONA     Of course not, darling.

GLORIA     Darling shit. I'll have your fucking head.

RAMONA     Let's look at this as a nice woman to woman discussion. Save your foul mouth for your gentlemen visitors.

GLORIA     Woman to woman? You're not even human. You're just bad energy looking for people who can recharge you.

RAMONA     And what are you, dear.

GLORIA     Younger. And better looking.

RAMONA     To borrow one of your expressions. Fuck you. Not that youth or appearance really mean very much to me. It's just that I refuse to let you avoid reality any longer.
       [*Pause*]

GLORIA     How come the boss doesn't have you followed.

RAMONA     Because I do not work for him. And you know that.

GLORIA     You've never said that.

RAMONA     Nevertheless you know it. And you've known it for quite some time. Yes or no?
       [**GLORIA** *shrugs*]

RAMONA     Ah well. What does it matter really.

GLORIA     Who cut off my sister's hand?

RAMONA     You did. Yes or no.

GLORIA  Yes or no?

RAMONA  Yes. You were in the midst of some fairly active drug-induced hysteria. Leslie was watching over you.

GLORIA  You're a lying whore.

RAMONA  You cut off her hand with a butcher's knife / You've never seen such a sight in your life / You poor ... dumb ... bitch.

GLORIA  Lying demented whore.

[GLORIA *turns away.* RAMONA *reaches out quickly. Grabs* GLORIA *by the hair*]

RAMONA  Don't turn away. Where are you going to go. Suppose this war never ends. That it just goes on and on in various disguises. A girl like you can't survive out there with the starving parasites and the deviates. And you know that. Your problem is that you have too much spirit. It's preventing you from doing what you know is best for a girl like you in times like these. Your spirit should be broken so that you can just relax give-up survive and occasionally make outrageous plans for something more. I know that's all you want, you see. Because we're so much alike.

[*She lets her go*]

GLORIA  We're nothing alike.

RAMONA  Admit what you did to your sister.

GLORIA  I can't. I don't remember.

RAMONA  You don't have to remember. I'm telling you.

GLORIA  But you lie.

RAMONA  Why were you in the cellar.

GLORIA  Punishment.

RAMONA  Yes. Because you asked to be punished.

GLORIA  No. Because —

RAMONA  Because of what you did to your sister you asked to be put in the cellar.

GLORIA  I don't remember.

RAMONA  Because you were taking drugs.

GLORIA  No, I've never taken —

RAMONA  Tell the truth now. You're not really writing a book are you. You're just keeping a silly little schoolgirl's diary.

GLORIA  I'm an artist.

RAMONA  Tell the truth now.

GLORIA  No I'm writing —

RAMONA    It's gone. The book was destroyed.

       [**GLORIA** *sits down*]

GLORIA    Did you read it first.

RAMONA    What for. Who wrote it.

GLORIA    Nobody. A silly little schoolgirl.

RAMONA    A silly little tarty schoolgirl.

GLORIA    Tarty.

RAMONA    Who cut off her sister's hand.

GLORIA    Cut it off. Cut it right off.

       [*Pause*]

RAMONA    There now. That's much better isn't it. I knew I could help you. And now that you've admitted it you can blame me. I don't mind. I'll take the blame forever. Just like I do for Miguel. Miguel just had to admit that he was responsible for Friedrich's accident and then he could relax like you're doing now. Because he knew I would take the blame. He was able to relax so much that he just disappeared. [*Smiles*]

       [*Pause*]

GLORIA    You've always liked Leslie better than me.

RAMONA    I like you both the same.

GLORIA    Love us?

RAMONA    Yes.

GLORIA    Are we leaving tonight?

RAMONA    Ah. That's better.

            [*Blackout*]

# Scene 13

RAMONA *and* COOK. RAMONA *pacing back and forth.*
*Businesslike.*
COOK *sitting on the bed.*

RAMONA  So you see the patient was merely looking for an outlet for all her feelings of guilt. I held the water back until the proper moment then removed the final obstacle.

COOK  Patient?

RAMONA  Patient, sir. Doctor, patient. Understand now?

COOK  No.

RAMONA  Christian psychology. Catholic analysis. The guilt and punishment ethic. I'm a lay practitioner. Studied informally at the convent. Portuguese orthodox. Hong Kong slightly unorthodox. Understand me now?

COOK  I'm sorry.

RAMONA  [*goes to closet*] Well something had to be done. I found myself surrounded by all these unhealthy people. [*Takes out a suit of clothes, hard to make out what exactly*] In my charge more or less. A lavish programme of therapy had to be worked out.
[*She goes behind dressing partition. Starts to change*]

COOK  Madame, I am waiting patiently for the truth.

RAMONA  Which one.

COOK  How many can there be.

RAMONA  How many do you want there to be.

COOK  Just one.

RAMONA  Which one is that?

COOK  The real one.

RAMONA  Which one is that.

COOK  Only you know.

RAMONA  A terrible responsibility. I don't know if I'm up to it.
[COOK *starts to write something in his notebook.* RAMONA *comes out from behind partition. She is dressed in a man's suit. Her hair tied up.* COOK *looks up*]

RAMONA  [*staring at him*] I mean I don't feel that I should have to do it alone.

[**COOK** *puts down his note pad.* **RAMONA** *smiles. Puts on her hat*]

[*Blackout*]
[*Music. Piano. Beginning slow. Almost melodic.
Gradually quickening. Becoming dissonant*]

## Scene 14

*Begins in darkness. A loud piercing laugh gradually gaining supremacy as the music fades.*
*Eventually the laughter becomes almost normal.*
*Lights. To suggest a smoke film.*
**SEBASTIAN**, *dressed in* **RAMONA**'s *bathrobe is packing.*
**LESLIE** *is laughing loudly. Then crying. Groaning in great pain.*
**GLORIA** *sits next to her slowly unscrewing her hook. They are both smoking opium*]

GLORIA     Does it hurt much?

LESLIE     Can't you get me something stronger.

GLORIA     There is nothing stronger.

LESLIE     Please!

GLORIA     Shush.

LESLIE     Please!!

GLORIA     Shush!

LESLIE     You're scraping my veins. Goddamn you.

GLORIA     Just a minute, baby.

LESLIE     Christ! My veins!

        [**GLORIA** *is pulling the hook out slowly*]

GLORIA     Here. Here.

LESLIE     Pull the fucking thing. You goddamn –

GLORIA     Here now.

LESLIE     – goddamn stinking –

GLORIA     Now now –

LESLIE     – stinking, stinking –

GLORIA     Now! [*She yanks it out*]

LESLIE     [*screams*] Slut!

SEBASTIAN     Here's a little number I picked up in Rome. A little too purple for the Orient. But I've just been dying to wear it.

        [**LESLIE** *has her head on* **GLORIA**'s *shoulder.* **GLORIA** *is rubbing her forehead*]

GLORIA     How's that.

        [**LESLIE** *is dazed*]

LESLIE     What?

GLORIA     How's that feel?

LESLIE      It hurts.

GLORIA      Love you. [*Hugs her*]

SEBASTIAN   Love you. [*Giggles*] Ah.

LESLIE      Why'd you take it out. Now I've only got a stump. You're always
            trying to hurt me.

GLORIA      Love you baby. That hook wasn't you. It wasn't real. It's you I
            love baby. Know that.

LESLIE      I know.

GLORIA      Know that? Please?

LESLIE      I said I know! [*Closes her eyes*]
                    [SEBASTIAN *takes this in. Goes over. Tenderly hugs them both*]

SEBASTIAN   Together always. Our little family. I think once we get to Casa-
            blanca I'll file adoption papers. Or custody papers or whatever it
            is I need to make you legitimate. To make you real. Wouldn't that
            be nice Gloria? To be real?

GLORIA      Yes.

SEBASTIAN   Yes mommy.

GLORIA      Yes mommy.

SEBASTIAN   If only Miguel were alive to see this. He always wanted dau-
            ghters, you know. He was so sensitive in that particular way.
            Everytime I think of him I feel like crying.

GLORIA      It's okay, mommy. Forget all that. I hate to see you sad.

SEBASTIAN   You remind one so much of your father. He hated to see me sad.
            Would do almost anything to avoid it. And you have his eyes.

GLORIA      You never told me that.

SEBASTIAN   I should have. We made so many mistakes. Little oversights. I
            had my hands full with your older brother, he was a bitter
            disappointment but even so — What time is it?

GLORIA      Twelve-thirty.

SEBASTIAN   Almost time to leave. [*Breaks away. Claps his hands*] Are you
            girls packed. This one sure is.

GLORIA      These are all the clothes we have.

SEBASTIAN   I forgot. Please don't say anything more about it though. I find it
            a trifle embarrassing.

LESLIE      We wouldn't even have these clothes if we hadn't gone to that
            school.

GLORIA      But remember Leslie it was mommy who forced us to go to that
            school.

SEBASTIAN    Please. Embarrassing.

GLORIA    It's okay. I know you'll take better care of us from now on.

SEBASTIAN    I promise I will. [*Crosses himself. Giggles*] Love you.

> [*A shot.* LESLIE *stands. Eyes wide open. Turns slowly to* SEBASTIAN]

LESLIE    You promised this wouldn't happen.

SEBASTIAN    I have to finish packing.

> [RAMONA *bursts through the door. Still in a man's suit. Now wearing lots of jewellry. Carrying a pistol. Skulks about in Sebastian's weak-kneed manner.* LESLIE *looks her over. Leaves*]

RAMONA    Why was I kept waiting. Answer my questions. I have rights. [*two hands on the pistol pointing it all around the room*] Who sent that stupid son of a bitch into my office. Which one of you little Catholic tramps sent that boy to rob me.

SEBASTIAN    We hope you didn't harm the young man.

RAMONA    I shot him in the legs. Left him bleeding to death on the floor.

SEBASTIAN    Oh you shouldn't have done that. It was just a little practical joke. Something to bring the family together again. Really daddy you have developed a terrible habit of overreacting to things. We know you've been under a lot of pressure. Fading away. Losing your identity. Whatever. But we count on our sense of humour to keep us all going. Now you just turn around and march right back in there and apologize to your son. Do you hear —

> [*He is interrupted by* RAMONA *who suddenly sticks her pistol in his mouth.* GLORIA *has been staring out the window. She sighs*]

*[Blackout]*

*[Strangely loud sound of someone eating something]*

*[Lights up]*

> [SEBASTIAN *has gone.* GLORIA *is still staring out the window.* RAMONA *is standing behind her. Holding a butcher's knife*]

GLORIA    Leslie is leaving. She's walking down the street. Left foot. Right foot. Cripples are pulling at the hem of her skirt. Soldiers are making passes at her. Old ladies are calling her names. But she just keeps walking. And she's walking very well. Oh yes, faster.

Faster. Left foot. Right foot. Left. I don't think she's coming
back. Daddy, did you steal my book? You know I've been
writing in that book for a long time.

[**RAMONA** *lays the knife on* **GLORIA**'s *throat*]

GLORIA    [*calmly*] Yes. I want you to kill me.

[*Pause*]

[*Blackout*]

[*Several highly amplified 'slitting' sounds. Pause. Spot on the
door.* **FRIEDRICH** *comes through. On his stumps. He takes a silk
handkerchief from his sleeve. Delicately wipes his brow. Puts the
handkerchief back*]

FRIEDRICH    [*apparently bored*] Oh dear. What will you do with me then.
Something quite perverse I imagine. [*Pause*] I hope. [*Smiles*]

[*Spot on* **RAMONA**]

RAMONA    Is your piano playing much improved, Friedrich.

MITCH    Yes mother. I practised daily. Even during the war I always
found time to play a little.

RAMONA    Then you'll be spared. I think we'll be better off. Just the two of
us.

[*Spot on* **COOK**]

COOK    Was that always your intention?

RAMONA    The questions must stop.

[*But* **COOK**'s *mind is somewhere else*]

COOK    Crimes have been committed. Behaviour is not what it once was.
The natural order of things has been severely twisted. The
suburbs of Hong Kong are not safe for the family unit. Foreign
substances are appearing in people's bloodstreams. The cannibals and the Cristians are uniting for the purpose of no-good.
It's ninety-two degrees Farenheit and decency and clear-headed
thinking might just be things of the past. [*Lights a cheroot*] Is it
possible that no one is safe?

[**FRIEDRICH** *makes his way toward the piano. All lights off.
Except for spot on* **RAMONA**]

RAMONA    I don't really care.

[*Long pause. As she waits for* **FRIEDRICH** *to reach the piano
and begin playing. The music. Soft. Melodic*]

RAMONA   I saw how pathetic he looked in the doorway. Blood dripping from his stumps. Wiping his forehead with that dreadful handkerchief. My little midget dandy. How could I kill him. Especially if it was true that he now played well. Especially since I knew it would be important to have music playing from now on. I mean once you have killed off all your family and then you have these boring feelings of guilt to deal with and once you have dealt with them and moved on to punishment which can be many things like taking to dangerous exotic drugs in huge amounts and once you've done that and done it well so as to bend your brain then what is there but to lie down in satin sheets and have music playing to you, into you forever. Except occasionally when the lizard comes to call. Then you must have silence so you can hear the reptile do his little hiss, his little tongue flicking insinuating sound in the night. You see Miguel was a monster in a black cloth sneaking into my little stone room with the bells still chiming in my ears and the mother superior two doors away and the son of god over my head. Whispering, sister I have something important to tell you. Father, you should not be here. Your ears are all red and your eyes are cloudy. Sister sit up. No stay still. I have a big dick to tell you, have you heard this story before. But stop him if you had. With my mind on my father dragging me down the road to the convent saying Ramona you'll like it here. They've got food and god is waiting to take care of you for always. Father you should not be here. Father. Marry me. Marry me and we'll go away. No don't marry me. I'm sick and I'll kill if you do. Some great bull promising to make it better by making me his wife. I will. I do. Just get me out of this blessed stinking prayer soaked dormitory where the brides of Christ lie waiting in little rows for their husband to arrive who by not arriving protects them from his arrival — and forgives us all at once for hoping anyway — Once I saw little Teresa my friend crouched in a corner after morning prayers afraid she was going to be locked in the closet again for wetting her pants. (These little girls in uniforms have such silly fears) and one of the sisters over her asking if the closet wasn't better than being sent home. Yes don't send me home, sister. My god don't ever send me home!

These little Catholic girls all black and white to the knee do such funny things, should never be let out to do their funny things. Jesus I woke up one day and he'd made me pregnant and I knew I had this two-headed crab-like creature in my belly. God's revenge Miguel, let's flush it out of me and bury it someplace. I kept having nightmare babies in my sleep. Once I gave birth to an Iroquois Indian who grew gigantic on my stomach and then assaulted me just like a picture I once had. Of an Iroquois Indian raping a demented pilgrim girl out by the wood pile. The pitiful demented little pilgrim girl too stupid to scream, one eye on his knife and the other on this terrifying growth between his legs. Scream you little moron. Scream till you make him shake. Then gouge out his eyes and take his own knife and carve him up into pieces. I was given that picture when I was eleven by my educated uncle and even then I knew the right approach to take to rape. It's kill or be killed. Fuck or get fucked and don't ever let me catch you crying afterward like that demented pilgrim. In fact, I had this thought once I'm going to rape a man. I'm going to follow him for hours with my eyes hanging all over his body and when I come to do it he won't enjoy it, not even a little but I'm going to keep asking him if he's enjoying it not even a little. Oh. Not even a little little? Just between us? Then you must be sick. [*Sniffs*] What's that odour? No one is safe. Behaviour is not what it once was. Oh this nightmare is real. It tells the story of − [*Stops. Sniffs*] Christians? [*Sniffs again*] Cannibals? [*More quickly*] The story of a family and Miguel's deterioration and how small he became and how he changed disguises. Priest to poppa to pimp, not that it was his idea, by the time he'd sunk to poppa he had no ideas and his mind was − [*She observes herself in the suit for the first time*] Oh look at this then. [*A couple of steps*] Very smart. Very strong. Oh yes this will do. [*Stops suddenly. Sniffs*] The lizard again. [*Looks over her shoulder*] Where?

[*Blackout*]


END

## NOTES

NOTES

NOTES

NOTES

**NOTES**

# NOTES